Beyond Compliance Design of a Quality System

Tools and Templates for Integrating Auditing Perspectives

Auditing titles from Quality Press

The Certified Quality Auditor, Fifth Edition
Ed. Lance B. Coleman Sr.

Advanced Quality Auditing
Lance B. Coleman Sr.

How to Audit ISO 9001:2015: A Handbook for Auditors
Chad Kymal

Also from Janet Bautista Smith

Auditing Beyond Compliance: Using the Portable Universal Quality Lean Auditing Model

The Art of Integrating Strategic Planning, Process Metrics, Risk Mitigation, and Auditing

New from Quality Press

Connected, Intelligent, Automated: The Definitive Guide to Digital Transformation and Quality 4.0
N. M. Radziwill

Culture Is Everything: How to Become a True Culture Warrior and Lead Your Organization to Victory
Jeff Veyera

Data Quality: Dimensions, Measurement, Strategy, Management, and Governance
Rupa Mahanti

Data Integrity and Compliance: A Primer for Medical Product Manufacturers
José Rodríguez-Pérez

Root Cause Analysis: The Core of Problem Solving and Corrective Action, Second Edition
Duke Okes

A Practical Field Guide for ISO 13485:2016: Medical Devices–Quality Management Systems–Requirements for Regulatory Purposes
Erik V. Myhrberg and Joseph Raciti, with Brandon L. Myhrberg

The ASQ Certified Quality Improvement Associate Handbook, Fourth Edition
Eds. Grace L. Duffy and Sandra L. Furterer

ISO 56000: Building an Innovation Management System: Bring Creativity and Curiosity to Your QMS
Peter Merrill

For more information on Quality Press titles, please visit our website at:
http://www.asq.org/quality-press

Beyond Compliance Design of a Quality System

Tools and Templates for Integrating Auditing Perspectives

———■　■　■———

Janet Bautista Smith
with Robert Alvarez

Quality Press
Milwaukee, Wisconsin

American Society for Quality, Quality Press, Milwaukee 53203
© 2020 by Janet Bautista Smith
All rights reserved. Published 2020
Printed in the United States of America

25 24 23 22 21 20   7 6 5 4 3 2 1

Publisher's Cataloging-in-Publication Data

Names: Smith, Janet Bautista, author. | Alvarez, Robert, contributor.
Title: Beyond compliance design of a quality system : tools and templates for
integrating auditing perspectives / Janet B. Smith ; Robert Alvarez.
Description: Includes bibliographical references and index. | Milwaukee, WI:
Quality Press, 2020.
Identifiers: LCCN 2020940659 | ISBN 978-1-951058-23-4 (pbk.) |
978-1-951058-24-1 (epub) | 978-1-951058-25-8 (pdf)
Subjects: LCSH Quality control—Auditing. | Auditing. | Total quality management.
| BISAC BUSINESS & ECONOMICS / Auditing | BUSINESS & ECONOMICS / Quality
Control | BUSINESS & ECONOMICS / Total Quality Management
Classification: LCC HF5667 .B268 2020 | DDC 657/.45—dc23

Publisher: Seiche Sanders
Managing Editor: Sharon Woodhouse
Sr. Creative Services Specialist: Randy L. Benson

ASQ advances individual, organizational, and community excellence worldwide
through learning, quality improvement, and knowledge exchange.

Bookstores, wholesalers, schools, libraries, businesses, and organizations: Quality
Press books are available at quantity discounts for bulk purchases for business,
trade, or educational uses. For more information, please contact Quality Press at
800-248-1946 or books@asq.org.

To place orders or browse the selection of all Quality Press titles, visit our website
at: http://www.asq.org/quality-press

 Printed on acid-free paper

Quality Press
600 N. Plankinton Ave.
Milwaukee, WI 53203-2914
Email: books@asq.org

ASQ   Excellence Through Quality™

This book is dedicated to
my son, Cosmo, and to Gaaelya.

– Janet Bautista Smith

Contents

List of Figures, Tables, and Templates

Figures

Tables

Templates

Preface

The development and maintenance of a quality management system (QMS) is based on many variables, such as company goals, market trends, company workforce, technology capability, and customer requirements (including quality/industry certifications like ISO, the U.S. Food and Drug Administration (FDA), military, etc.).

This book provides case studies, models, and templates on selected core elements that are common in the quality field, based on the combined perspectives and hands-on experiences of the quality system designer and internal and external auditors. This unique combination of real-life lessons learned can be easily applied in any industry regardless of size, product, or service.

The validity and effectiveness of the models presented in this book have been scrutinized and accepted by customers and auditors in manufacturing, government, and service businesses, and in environments as varied as medical devices, automotive, military, and customs security. The models and case studies compiled by the author come from years of hands-on experiences, reflecting the two sides of an audit—that of the quality system designer, or the auditee, and that of the external auditor.

Validation of a Quality Management System

One common source of QMS validation is the integration of available information, such as the internet or published documents, in the design of a quality system. These may be good sources, but they are almost always based on a one-sided view, that is, the voice of the quality system designer (e.g., quality assurance (QA) management or a consultant) sharing the lessons learned throughout the design and deployment of a system. The limitation of these sources introduces the possibility of biased input. One can design a million-dollar quality system, but if it is not effective or efficient, it is not worth a cent.

So, how does one validate a quality system's efficacy? One unbiased measure of success for validating a quality system is the evaluation of customers and/or external auditors such as ISO auditors, the FDA, etc.

The concept of enhancing results through the merging of views and expertise in collaboration was also explored in a paper called "Lessons Learned from Employing Multiple Perspectives in a Collaborative Virtual Environment for Visualizing Data" (Park, Kapoor, and Leigh 2000):

> "Reapplying important lessons to prevent future mistakes is a core reason why organizations capture lessons learned. Although the concept of lessons learned has evolved into a formal and structured management practice, as an idea, the practice of capturing and archiving knowledge is not new. Using this practice involves performing two essential activities: capturing important lessons learned and making effective use of these."

Why reinvent models when you can reference time-tested, ageless concepts already polished through years of scrutiny from both customers and external party audits? Sharing these techniques and lessons learned from two perspectives is what makes this book different from other published documents in this domain.

Acknowledgments

Janet Smith

My gratitude to my husband, Chet, and my son, Cosmo, for their patience and inspirational support while I burned the midnight oil during the completion of this project.

I also thank my sister, Cynthia Santos, and my nephew, Bryan Santos, who provided support reflected by their positive interest and enthusiasm on the project.

Many thanks to my friends Xin Xiang and Andrew Welling, whose friendship included keeping me healthy by walking with me for fresh air or eating a meal with me during lunch breaks for a change of scenery. These friends also went above and beyond work by providing valuable critique to my various hobby art projects. I also thank my friends Sandy Nix and Joy Hannan for providing encouraging support for this project.

I am also grateful to my "plant buddies" who added beautiful plants to my office. We shared and exchanged interesting plant challenges. They are: Lynn Russell, Mary Kavette, Sharon Crouch, Todd Hoehn, and others.

My gratitude goes to my quality assurance team and friends (Rodolfo Nava, Ramiro Chacon, Victor Garcia, Jorge Molina, and Mariann Kay) for diligently working with me in the creation and execution of quality initiatives in support of compliance and continuous improvement. They are always available to lend a hand with a smile. Thanks to the ProTrans family: Craig Roeder, Gary Cardenas, Shawn Masters, Ratnam Philip, Lisa Doerner, Chris Blunk, Kathy Joy, Riley McGaughey, Benjamin Mathis, Barbara Carothers, Eracleo Vallejo, Jeremy Garrett, Bradford C. Smoot, George Gephart, Joe Garcia, Paul Chiszar, Marco Prieto, and many others for supporting the deployment and integration of quality programs in the ProTrans Quality Management System. It was an enjoyable journey.

The American Society for Quality (ASQ) organization is a critical platform for sharing knowledge such as the publication of this book—many thanks to the dedicated leadership, divisions, and members in maintaining this portal as a contributor to the society's growth. Special thanks to the peer reviewers and ASQ's staff in providing dedicated guidance in completing this book.

Robert Alvarez

The journey of being a quality assurance professional is without destination. Although I have excelled in my profession, I acknowledge the countless ASQ members, mentors, supervisors, and peers that have supported me in achieving such a level of competence. As a result of this, it is with this competence, that I enthusiastically share my knowledge, guidance, and experiences, in the hope of facilitating a career path for future individuals in pursuing such an extremely rewarding profession.

1

Creation of Quality Management Systems (QMS) Reflecting the Two Sides of Auditing: The QMS Designer's and the External Auditor's Perspectives

The design of a *perfect* quality management system (QMS) is one of the quality goals and the crowning glory of a QMS designer (typically the function of a quality team). A QMS designer can create a quality management program purportedly worth a million dollars and in full compliance with the designer's own requirements, and, yet, if the QMS is not aligned with the expectations of the stakeholders—management, customers, business partners, etc.—then it is not worth a cent.

The million-dollar question, then, is, "What are some indicators that will help show the QMS design's successful alignment with the stakeholders' requirements and expectations?"

The validation of the QMS by internal and external compliance audits is one of the most visible and dynamic ways of achieving that stamp of certification and implementation of the industry's best practices. Audit validation of the QMS as the path to implementing best practices is the focus of this book. What follows is dedicated to sharing lessons learned in the deployment of time-tested QMS systems from both the QMS designer's and the auditors' experiences. This holistic perspective benefits both beginners and advanced quality professionals.

External audit certification of a QMS model (i.e., quality certification under an industry standard from ISO, FDA, a military organization, environmental agencies, etc.) offers added validation of a system's effectiveness and increases a company's market competitiveness. There are many variations of the QMS model, but which one has the highest rate of success? The optimal QMS model for a situation depends on many variables, such as company vision, resource availability, market competition, regulatory requirements, etc.

1

This chapter offers samples and guidelines in the selection of the QMS elements that are easy to create and have been validated through years of implementation and audit verifications.

Figure 1.1 is a pictorial model of a QMS created and implemented by QMS designer and author Janet Smith, during her more than 35 years of quality management employments in various industries, including medical device and automotive manufacturing, design environments, and logistics. A company's goals and strategies may change, depending on management's direction, but the core flow remains the same. This core design is time tested, with a proven record of effectiveness through audit validations by the FDA, military, ISO, TS (automotive standard), AS (aerospace standard), C-TPAT (Customs Trade Partnership Against Terrorism, U.S. Customs and Border Protection), and other auditors.

Robert Alvarez, an external auditor associated with a registrar for more than 25 years, provided review during the development of this project. Alvarez's feedback to QMS designers, including Janet Smith, during his quality certification audits has been a valuable tool in the continuing improvement of their QMS's effectiveness.

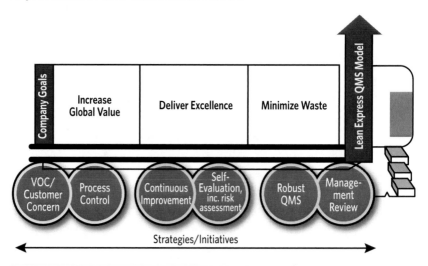

Figure 1.1 The Lean Express: example of a QMS showing typical QMS elements. This model, implemented and validated by internal and external audits, reflects typical business missions and strategies, and can be applied to most industries with adjustments for their company-specific requirements. It reflects the QMS designer's and the auditor's perspectives—the two faces of auditing merged to forge a strong and timeless quality tool.

(Smith 2010)

The model in Figure 1.1 is just one of many QMS design possibilities based on the vision of a company's stakeholders. Following are some guidelines for starting your own customized QMS design:

Step 1: Define the company's vision or management's strategic plan.

How do you get this information? Asking your manager, management, or chief executive officer (CEO) is one direct approach; however, employing the method that makes the most sense for your company's hierarchy may be a better approach. In the example, the company's goals were defined as:

- Increase global value
- Deliver excellence
- Reduce costs, and minimize waste and defects

Step 2: Once the vision or company goals are identified, list the potential strategies to support the goals.

Imagine these goals as freight to be loaded onto the express train as cargo. The train wheels are the supporting initiatives that will carry the cargo to the destination. The chosen strategies for the example, the company strategies that will help it reach its goals (destination), are:

- Voice of the customer (VOC), such as customer feedback
- Process control
- Continuous improvement
- Self-evaluation
- Robust QMS
- Management review

Step 3: Identify the initiatives to support the strategies.

Once strategies to support the vision are selected, as shown previously, then the company can start identifying the feasible initiatives to support the strategies. Some examples are shown in Table 1.1.

Examples of strategies to support company goals	Examples of initiatives to support the strategies	Examples of effectiveness indicators
VOC	Customer feedback system	• Benchmark for tracking progress • Trend of customer complaints per period (for example, monthly comparison to identify any trends for further investigation)
Process control	Inspection program	• Error rate per core (first pass yield) • Trends of findings in internal evaluations (Are there repeating issues? Why?) • Productivity (e.g., overtime may be an indicator of process issues)
Continuous improvement	Gap analysis on selected core process performance trends to identify improvement (e.g., recurring inspection findings)	• Measure success by error reduction and/or cost savings (Note: Cost savings can include cycle time or waste reduction through process streamlining.)
Self-evaluation	Internal audit program	• Cost of quality versus benefits. (e.g., cost of inspection program versus reduction of errors, customer complaints/ returns, etc.)
Robust QMS	Develop achievable metrics as performance indicators so QMS's effectiveness is continually monitored or adjusted as needed, including reaction to risks.	• Layered metrics to measure performance (Note: Layered metrics act as a pre-alert before the occurrence of a significant and possibly irreversible event. For example: On-time delivery is the core metric, but within this metric there are components such as planning, pick-up, and actual delivery processes that should also be given metrics.)

Table 1.1 Examples of initiatives to support and manage strategies, with effectiveness indicators.

Lessons Learned

Following are some basic pillars for creating a sustainable QMS and measuring its effectiveness:

Secure management commitment. Buy-in needs to be secured, structured, visible to the workforce, and demonstrate verifiable evidence of implementation at all levels of the system; otherwise, the QMS will not be supported and will eventually collapse.

One technique of securing this piece at the outset is to create a document outlining management's required involvement in the program. Having the document is not enough; it must be read, understood, and approved by the designated management (e.g., CEO or vice-president level). The documented information can be a simple flowchart showing the needed elements of management's interaction, with things such as participation in management review events, escalation point on roadblocks, etc. In this way, their participation will be well structured and visible to the workforce. An approved management assignee may be considered depending on the company's hierarchy structure and various restrictions on management (e.g., travel schedules, alternate locations, etc.).

It has been proven through actual observation that, in some cases, human nature can be resistant to change! As part of unlocking this resistance, it helps to have an official written procedure backed by management, in addition to a clear explanation of the benefits that will be gained if change is embraced. Cultivation of a quality culture that is compatible with the stakeholders' vision and requirements is key in the success of the company's goals supported by the workforce's commitment. The quality culture nurtured by an organization is unique to the organization's needs and must be developed and supported by the organization's leadership—it is not one size fits all. There is much published information on this topic that may be used as reference for developing or gathering information on quality culture, such as the following:

- "Apple Inc.'s organizational culture is a key factor in the continuing success of the business. A company's organizational or corporate culture establishes and maintains the business philosophy, values, beliefs, and related behaviors among employees. For example, the company's cultural traits are aligned with the drive for innovation, which is a major factor that determines business competitiveness..." (Meyer 2019)

- "Google's cultural features are focused on enhancing employee performance. The company expects effective motivation through its organizational culture. For example, in developing solutions to target customers' everyday problems, Google's corporate culture motivates workers to think outside the box and aim for novel ideas..." (Smithson 2018)

Start simple. It is easy to get buy-in if the initiatives are simple, cost effective, and have measurable added value for the stakeholders.

Use existing resources as possible to achieve minimum initiatives in line with the company's goals. After the initial phase of implementation, the program should be re-evaluated for any adjustments that may be needed (e.g., measured effectiveness, resource allocation, etc).

One way of starting simple is to gather or create basic process flowcharts depicting the core processes. This will provide visibility of the rough scope to be covered by the QMS. The basic process flowchart can be further drilled down to the subprocesses under the core process.

Show quantified and verifiable results. Demonstrate expected measurable results, including savings, as performance metrics catch attention.

Simple reports on cost avoidance or returns due to effective error prevention or risk discovery initiatives are some examples of quantifying savings. These activities do not require massive resources or high technology and can be easily accomplished. Again, start simple—do not aim for a complex report requiring data that are difficult to obtain; this can be done in the later part of the program.

In reporting measured results (e.g., process yield), benchmark and target values should be stated as clearly as possible to fully assess progress.

Validate the initiatives. Validate the initiatives included in the QMS in a small, manageable pilot run involving process owners. Do this to obtain buy-in and to get feedback on what's critical-to-quality to ensure success.

This process provides insight into the feasibility of achieving the broader goals and aids in defining the acceptance criteria. It should be noted that, in some cases, validation results with values lower than the targeted goal may still be released as "approved" under limited parameters (e.g., defining acceptance criteria). This practice depends on many variables and risks, with considerations including legal impact, safety, customer satisfaction, approval hierarchy, an emergency situation such as a global pandemic, etc. The validation process also needs a proper structured review and approval protocol to ensure safety, efficacy, and compliance with the rules or governing authority as needed (e.g., the FDA, in addition to an internal team such as a technical review board or similar entity).

Review the pilot run results. Review these results both with management and at the grassroots level (workforce) to get different perspectives and improvement input.

Apply the plan-do-check-act (PDCA) model. Using PDCA means validations or pilot runs may be performed multiple times to verify the results until an acceptable level is reached.

Solicit input from the different business units of the system. This can be achieved in many ways depending on the complexity and size of the company. Solicitation of input may include surveys, site visits, conference interviews, etc. Consider reviewing all the core or critical processes for each business unit to attain knowledge about each business unit's purpose, interrelationships, and impact on the QMS elements. Choose the most logical, cost-efficient, and effective method to fit the situation.

Remember, the QMS is a living document that will be deployed to cover all the business units; therefore, representation from the various parts of the system is critical for full coverage. For example, if the QMS is based on FDA standards, elements of this standard should be reviewed to determine how they can be incorporated into the business unit. For example, if the business unit under evaluation is the labeling department, the focus should be on the FDA standard elements involving labeling, such as a traceability system, the archiving or removal of obsolete material, line clearance, the prevention of mix-ups, change management, etc.

Document all changes. Document all changes, even during the pilot runs, to ensure historical archiving of lessons learned in fine tuning the program.

Keep management and appropriate teams updated. This guarantees progress is tracked and proper credit is given to achievements contributed by the teams.

Give credit where it is due, regardless of contribution size. Avoid pooling all project initiatives under one bin. When all reporting is done by the project leader or manager, he or she may inadvertently mask the many individual efforts and contributions to the project. It is best to break down the major tasks and accomplishments so proper teams are given due credit; otherwise, this situation, if left unchecked, may yield bitterness on the teams and fuel a no buy-in attitude (e.g., "Why should we work hard to complete the task—we do all the leg work and data mining without credit, but the project manager gets the recognition, applause, and appreciation?"). This scenario may seem too trivial to be a cause for concern, but treating your workforce with the appropriate level of sensitivity has a great impact on morale, motivation, loyalty to the company, and productivity.

If you successfully tend to these basic pillars, you stand a pronounced chance of creating an effective and sustainable QMS.

Encourage continuing engagement of various workforce levels in creating or improving the QMS. Process owners' voices are excellent sources of improvement ideas in the creation or maintenance of a QMS. The process-owner level, which refers to the hands-on level (e.g., an assembly inspector), has the subject expertise on the process, roadblocks, and visibility of improvement opportunities impacting a business unit. Once the workforce is engaged in this initiative, there is no limit to how the different levels of the workforce can contribute in the continual improvement of the QMS. True, deep-rooted management commitment and leadership will open the doors to these opportunities to allow the two-way flow of effective communication. This two-way system further cultivates the workforce's buy-in, one of the critical factors of a dynamic QMS.

The highlights contained in this chapter are applicable for:

- Creation of a new QMS
- Maintenance or improvement of an existing QMS
- Modification or repair of a "broken" QMS

Do not reinvent the wheel! As mentioned, the quality models in this book have been deployed in many businesses and organizations and fine-tuned to withstand the test of time by internal and external auditors under the quality standards of different industries. The models may be easily adjusted to custom fit any type of business, quality standard in use, customer base, budget allocation, etc.

> "I believe that this is a good practice, and have strongly advocated for years that finding, assessing, and implementing best-practice is not only rational, but often moves an institution ahead more quickly in the marketplace."
>
> — Jim Benté, Vice President, Planning and
> Institutional Effectiveness, College of DuPage, Glen Ellyn, IL

Auditor's Perspective

The previous discussion focused on the QMS designer's perspective in the creation of an efficient and effective QMS expected by the stakeholders. The other side of auditing is the auditor's independent viewpoint and interpretation of the QMS program's compliance with the intent of the standards governing the QMS. The designed QMS may have the basic elements, such as those discussed previously, but may still be deemed as ineffective or lacking compliance by the auditor due to certain criteria. Part of the auditor's role is the use of certain indicators to ensure the QMS aligns with the auditor's perspectives. Some examples of these indicators are:

A QMS program may be deemed as lacking consistent deployment or measurement; therefore, it is ineffective.

There are many reasons for the intermittent deployment of a QMS, such as software change, etc. This can be easily detected by the auditor by reviewing certain indicators, such as performance trends for the last 6 or 12 months of data; significant fluctuations of data will be a flag for this noncompliance.

There should be a contingency plan to mitigate any disturbance in the system (e.g., software change) to achieve a seamless system. For example, there should be an alternative data collection method in metrics measurement if the data collection tool (e.g., software) is under a prolonged evaluation. In this example, stopping the data collection due to the software delay is not the solution; otherwise, discontinuing the collection may send a message that the metrics monitoring is not important. An alternative or equivalent initiative must be developed; otherwise, why collect the data?

A QMS program may be concluded as static without a periodic or structured review program.

The QMS program should incorporate a structured and periodic assessment of the QMS elements to ensure a continuing balance of the system. One way an auditor spots this weakness is through a review of a customer's original contract agreement versus the process change logs or history. There should be no gap between these reference documents that could significantly impact customer satisfaction. A concrete example is the removal of a customer requirement for labeling verification during the shipment process due to a software process update allowing verification of the label at the beginning of the order process. Although the change was a better early-error prevention/detection method, the original requirement on the QMS (i.e., label verification during the shipping process) was not updated. Thus, technically, the process, although lean, cost effective, and more effective, is noncompliant to the QMS documentation.

2

Measurement of the QMS Effectiveness and Alignment with the Auditor's Perspective Using Layered Metrics

It is not uncommon to get a deer-in-headlights response when asking a poor soul working at his or her station for the first time, "What are your quality objectives?" The company's quality objectives are often an abstract concept, especially for employees who have not previously been exposed to external audits (customer or regulatory). However, this is a simple question that the entire workforce should be able to answer at any given time regardless of who is asking the question. Why, then, is this not always the case?

Some teams may state, "Not my job! That's a management problem." This may seem logical: The identification of the business direction is management's main responsibility; therefore, the resulting actions of leadership within the organization (whether they fall under quality assurance, engineering, or other departments) are under management's domain. But such an explanation is no valid justification for a frozen-in-place look from the workforce. Rather, it possibly indicates that management may not have properly communicated, or failed delegation of relaying, this information through the ranks.

Management has the responsibility of communicating the meaning of the quality objectives to all reaches of the organization in a simple and comprehensible manner to encourage and support workforce buy-in. The business unit authorized by management to develop the QMS is typically designated as the responsible functionary for training the workforce in the vital elements of the QMS.

Now that the responsibility has been identified, this chapter can begin its discussion on the creation, execution, and monitoring of the quality objectives.

Questions About Quality Objectives

First, the following questions need to be answered to remove any mysticism shrouding quality objectives:

What is a quality objective?

One straightforward definition of a quality objective is the expectation of the stakeholders. It can be a high-level, overall quality objective (e.g., capture at least 40 percent of product X's market in five years), or it can be a compartmentalized or layered quality objective, such as metrics for all the subprocesses (e.g., pick-up of freight goal is 98 percent completion with a utilization goal of 85 percent to meet the overall delivery goal of 98 percent) or individual workers' performance (e.g., efficiency, tolerance of error rate, etc.).

Who is responsible for defining the quality objective values?

Typically, management or stakeholders, with input from the area leadership or subject experts, assign the initial values for quality objectives. These values may change during validation or over time due to process variables such as process changes, skill-set development, technology, or customer requirements. Thus, it is critical to continue validating the quality objectives to ensure alignment with the process variables.

This viewpoint is not limited to companies; it may be applied to a larger scope such as a global scenario. For example, in a global pandemic situation, the quality objective values expected from treatment drugs may be defined by the world leaders (e.g., World Health Organization) with input from subject experts such as leading scientists involved in the treatment task force.

Are quality objectives necessary to run a business?

Quality objectives are the core indicators of any process, as they measure its successes and identify its opportunities for improvement—everything from the simplest to the most complex variables. Take, for example, that an airplane's ability to meet its flight schedule is a quality objective measurement of the airline's competitiveness in the market; a medical device manufacturer's capacity to meet its customers' tolerances is key to ensuring the safety of the end users of its devices (and, thus, the company being able to stay in business).

Is it enough to identify the quality objectives for the key processes?

Identifying the quality objectives for the key processes is not enough. There also must be a pre-alert system to detect the start of any downward trends of the system's performance. No business entity wants a catastrophic surprise if the quality objectives fail without warning, without a chance to mitigate and reverse the situation. One way of doing this is through the use of layered metrics that are embedded in the quality objectives associated with the core processes.

Quality Objectives Using Layered Metrics

Layered metrics may be used to measure process performance functions and serve as a pre-alert notification of possible failure. This mechanism should be part of the process performance design for early detection and mitigation of issues in a QMS.

Pre-alert methods vary depending on the complexity of the process. In general, they can be quite simple to create; it only requires an understanding of the core processes and the associated interrelationship with the subprocesses' requirements to fully support the performance via metrics.

Consider this scenario as a way to understand the value of layered metrics: A restaurant chef's final measure of success is the presentation of a delicious meal served within a reasonable amount of waiting time for the customer, resulting in the customer's ultimate delight. How is this accomplished, reliably and repeatably, for every customer?

The following layers of metrics, presented in Table 2.1 and naming just a few for demonstration, are beneficial in achieving the chef's ultimate goal of customer satisfaction. Without these layers, it would be difficult to predict the consistent attainment of customer satisfaction in serving timely, delicious meals. None of these key variables can suddenly fail without warning (e.g., the shortage of a key ingredient, undetected until a customer places an order requiring that ingredient). Simply put, heading off such surprises is the value of layered metrics.

Layering the process metrics, as shown in Table 2.1, provides visibility of the subprocesses' performance and gives the opportunity to deploy root cause analysis or mitigation (including adjustment of metrics) to ward off a potential failure.

Subprocess	Potential layered metrics
Procurement's selection of dependable vendors	On-time delivery of materials
Verification of quality by raw material receivers and inspectors of incoming material	Frequency of rejected material due to quality concerns of the assistant chef during the selection from inventory
Stock of fresh materials in storage, readily available for use	Consistency of material inventory's safety stock level
Selection by the assistant chef of the right materials for meal preparation	Cycle time for picking the materials from inventory and completion of preparation for chef's final preparation
Dependable oven, properly calibrated for consistency	Oven performance (e.g., consistency)
Use of the right recipe	Scrap rate
Servers' accuracy in serving the right food to the right customer	Number of returned orders
Chef's reputation	Customer satisfaction

Table 2.1 Layered metrics—restaurant quality example.

Table 2.2, which may be used as a template, is another example of layered metrics, this one from a manufacturing environment.

In some cases, the layered metrics of monitoring quality objectives come in an unconventional format. One example is the use of waste avoidance as the success measurement instead of process performance. Waste avoidance is fairly easy to deploy, as waste is present in almost all aspects of any system. Waste avoidance as a method of quantifying the success of a quality objective is beneficial, especially if there is no other direct way of measuring the success rate.

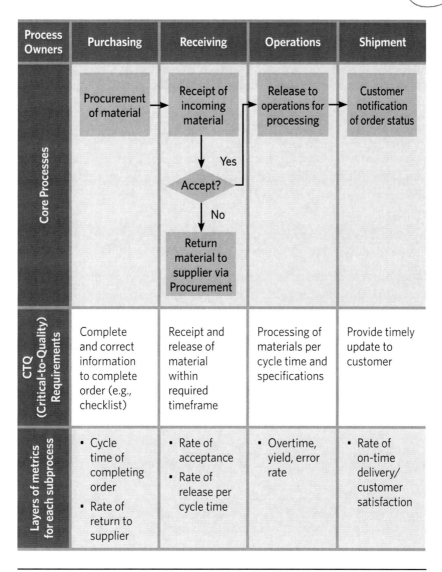

Process Owners	Purchasing	Receiving	Operations	Shipment
Core Processes	Procurement of material	Receipt of incoming material Accept? → Yes ↓ No Return material to supplier via Procurement	Release to operations for processing	Customer notification of order status
CTQ (Critical-to-Quality) Requirements	Complete and correct information to complete order (e.g., checklist)	Receipt and release of material within required timeframe	Processing of materials per cycle time and specifications	Provide timely update to customer
Layers of metrics for each subprocess	• Cycle time of completing order • Rate of return to supplier	• Rate of acceptance • Rate of release per cycle time	• Overtime, yield, error rate	• Rate of on-time delivery/ customer satisfaction

Table 2.2 Dynamic and layered metrics.

Example:

The following scenario shows the quantification of wasted time as a measure of the quality objective (i.e., communication's effectiveness), providing an opportunity to use this metric as a benchmark for improvement opportunity.

First, what do emails, popcorn, and tsunamis have in common?

As heat increases, kernel popping peaks, and the scrambling activity accelerates like a tsunami. If not carefully watched, the popcorn kernels may burn, create that awful smell, start smoking, and trigger a fire alarm (waste). This popcorn-tsunami analogy[1] is similar to email strings, as shown in the following example:

Company ABC's practice of forwarding a complaint to all process owners was analyzed as part of a streamlining initiative:

Identification of waste. It was determined that the average number of workers in this type of email distribution was 50, even though only five employees had the ability to investigate a complaint.

Deliverable or quality objective. Quantify waste and reduce it by at least 50 percent:

- Limit the email distribution to personnel who are directly responsible for processing the complaint.
- Create a central repository to archive all complaints to minimize email distribution and provide information access.

Measures of success. Measure of email waste and savings after implementation of initiative are shown in Table 2.3.

---

[1] J. Smith, "An Email and Popcorn and Tsunami Analogy," iSixSigma.com, https://www.isixsigma.com/community/blogs/an-email-and-popcorn-and-tsunami-analogy/

	Number of people receiving an email before the streamlining initiative	Number of people receiving an email after the streamlining initiative	Savings based on the frequency of five complaints emails per week
	100	5	
Average time to read each email: 0.5 minutes	Total time for 100 people to read one email: 50 minutes	Total time for 5 people to read one email: 2.5 minutes	237 minutes per week, or 205 hours per year

Table 2.3 Measure of email waste and savings after implementation of continuous improvement initiative.

Lessons Learned

There are many ways of measuring the success of a process performance using the layered metrics method described in this chapter. One needs to recognize the subprocesses and the supporting variables. Measure what matters!

- Layered metrics need to represent the interest of the stakeholders and should not be biased to focus on personal gain that may mislead the true performance of the process. One prevention tool is the use of secondary metrics.
- Metrics collected should trigger some actions, including improvement; otherwise, it is a waste of time if data remain static.
- Metrics should always be rereviewed in a logical frequency, especially if there are changes that impact performance.
- Performance metrics consistently exceeding or failing expectations need to be rereviewed to ensure metrics are still aligned with the requirements.

Following are some more examples of layered metrics:

On-time delivery metric. Layered metrics may include process cycle time compliance for core processes supporting on-time delivery. A performance of time study for each subprocess cycle between shifts will help determine a benchmark for the unit level of effort (ULE) or productivity measure. The variance may be the cause of overall on-time delivery failure, therefore providing visibility of the problematic area.

Manufacturing yield. Layered metrics may include the error rate of each assembly line as an indicator of productivity, training effectiveness, or a need to clarify procedures. Identifying the problematic line will help focus improvement efforts to improve overall yield.

Auditor's Perspective

As noted earlier, the auditor's role includes the use of various performance indicators to assess an initiative's compliance and effectiveness. It is not enough that quality objectives or metrics are identified and measured; the QMS may still fail the auditor's evaluation as viewed under a different perspective, for example:

Quality objectives may be known to management, but there is no drill down of knowledge to the workforce to ensure support and effectiveness.

The auditor can easily assess the overall effectiveness of the company's initiatives in supporting the major company goals simply by using one of the auditor's tools, such as verifying a high-level process flow during the audit. The first indicator of ineffective process monitoring is displayed by the random goals set by the department or business units. The metrics selected should have relevance to the ultimate goal (this is the concept of layered metrics discussed in this chapter). For example, if Assembly A's company-dictated goal is on-time delivery, the supporting department or business unit should have metrics associated with this major goal, such as cycle time of order completion, efficiency level, error rate due to training inefficiency, machine downtime/uptime, poor planning due to lack of insight/unqualified department leadership skill set, etc., all of which can ultimately impact the on-time delivery goal. The selection of effective metrics is one indication of the workforce's understanding and embrace of the company's vision or goal.

3

Customer Feedback
and the QMS

◾──◾

The objective of this chapter is to offer a path for utilizing customer feedback as a tool for operational excellence and as an additional pillar to the QMS. The analysis model in this chapter is based on the Lean and Six Sigma (LSS) concept being incorporated into the QMS using the define, measure, analyze, improve, and control (DMAIC) flow.[2]

Some customer feedback or risk may not necessarily be covered in the original QMS design for many reasons, such as change in customer needs, market trends, technology update, catastrophe-driven changes in business policies, etc. The beauty of a dynamic QMS is the feature of flexibility embedded in the QMS design to handle changes, including input from the customer feedback. One typical tool in updating the QMS is via a change control program wherein changes are properly evaluated for risk (e.g., FDA approval of a medical device modification or virus testing change, etc.), validated, approved for implementation, and monitored for efficacy and effectiveness. The QMS is a living element that does not remain static.

This timeless approach has been an integral part of QMS design regardless of business type or quality standard governing the company. The methodology's continual validation and refinement through the integration of customer feedback (sometimes referred to as customer complaints) and audits' acceptance make this a valuable tool worth sharing with the quality community.

---

[2] One does not have be an LSS expert to understand and deploy this model; LSS and DMAIC concepts are only mentioned to provide the readers the origin of this information flow.

Highlights of the DMAIC Analysis Model

- Define the problem to ensure proper root cause analysis. Simple tools such as the 5 Whys analysis, available in many publications, will help in getting the primary issue.

- Measure the benchmark. This includes the risk involved (e.g., 50 percent of inspected units are observed with cosmetic defect x, exceeding the tolerance for that product line for the week).

- Analyze the data, including quantifying the benefits of resolution identified by the root cause analysis. These actions should align with the identified problem.

- Measure the deliverables. Without measurement, it is difficult to assess success.

- Deploy the improvement. This is the application of lessons learned, not only on the problem area, but also on associated processes, products, and/or business units/workforce involved.

- Control the parameters that were developed during the improvement stage to keep sustainability until the next review cycle to identify improvement opportunities.

Common Pitfalls of Customer Complaints Processing

Figure 3.1 depicts some pitfalls of customer complaints processing. Understanding these pitfalls will help provide insight in converting these elements to customer satisfaction.

Figure 3.1 Customer complaints—examples of common causes.

Table 3.1 shows several common causes of unresolved or recurring customer complaints and recommended actions from an integrated auditing perspective. This table provides insight in understanding and converting customer dissatisfaction into continuous improvement initiatives.

Common causes of unresolved or recurring complaints	Recommended action
Incorrect "diagnosis" of the problem; wrong root cause. Consider where there may be tunnel vision, meaning other logical options may have been discarded due to a lack of knowledge or bias.	Rereview the problem, root cause, and action—do they align? One method is to think backwards. Focus on the expected output, and then ask: What is preventing the process from attaining this output? Select the top three causes. This question will open the door to view the roadblocks and root causes, as well as the evaluation of the appropriate action.
Vague plan; no measurable deliverables. A mentality of "It will work, trust me!" is often a reflection of having no commitment or measurement of success.	Involve process owners to get buy-in in seeing the benefits of improving the process. Generally, process owners want to do the best they can to accomplish the job; dealing with daily roadblocks is the least of their favorite tasks. Once this buy-in is achieved, the process owner will be a prime resource in identifying success metrics. Go a step further and quantify other benefits, such as time saved; error prevention to avoid rework or scrap rate that is an "eyesore" to the financial statement; and customer satisfaction.
No accountability and no time frame. This is a moving target problem, meaning no one owns the issue or action.	Increase the visibility of the initiative and, if appropriate, involve supervision level or management. This technique is sometimes called "peer pressure"—it may sound negative, but in some cases, it can be used as a positive tool to increase accountability and ownership. To increase positive effect, ensure the involved parties are aware of this visibility component and stress that the purpose is to keep communication open so no one is blindsided.

Table 3.1 Customer complaints and recommended actions.   *(continued)*

Common causes of unresolved or recurring complaints	Recommended action
No verification of effectiveness. Think of this as the "fireworks effect," meaning actions sound logical but cannot be verified.	If action cannot be verified or measured, it is a wasted effort, and there is the risk-of-repeat issue as well. Before signing off on action plans, the authorized gatekeeper of verification (typically, the QA team), needs to ensure there is a listed deliverable (i.e., evidence of success in corrective actions).
The improvement plan is a "band-aid." This is a containment plan and one that is not integrated into the system to prevent issue reoccurrence. (No buy-in from the grassroot or workforce level).	Containment plans or "band-aid" solutions do not necessarily resolve the issue permanently, but they are sometimes used as temporary mitigations. Therefore, it is critical to follow up after the containment period to ensure evidence of permanent action.
Process capability cannot support the customer requirement. Something was not detected during the contract review, or a gap was intentionally skipped with the intention of bridging it later.	Development of process capability metrics is one method of monitoring the process performance against the customer requirements. If there are already metrics in place, periodically rereview the metrics versus process changes or customer requirements to ensure alignment. One simple way is making this activity part of the account review on a periodic basis to ensure there is no "scope creep," meaning additional requirements have been added without proper change evaluations. How can these risks be detected or mitigated in a timely manner? There are many ways, including using a validation approval system, process monitoring using metrics as an indicator of success or trends, etc. This type of challenge typically begins during a contract review; perhaps it is the eagerness to win the bid, or lack of a skill set, knowledge, or experience in process analysis to identify and prevent potential issues.

Table 3.1 Customer complaints and recommended actions.

Converting Customer Feedback into Operational Excellence

Recognize the positive side of customer complaints.

Looking at the glass of water as "half full" instead of "half empty" is a foundational discipline that can help an entire organization view and use complaints as an opportunity to learn and grow. Not recognizing these growth experiences is a common mistake most management teams fail to leverage, without realizing the impact on the process owners' motivation and empowerment.

Some complaints may initiate a major improvement need, requiring asset allocation. This may not be a problem for brand-name or large corporations (e.g., Apple), but small-to-medium-sized companies may not necessarily have this luxury. For small-to-medium-sized businesses, achievement of changes, including those that are initiated by complaints, may have to happen on an incremental basis due to asset constraint. With that said, these companies may deploy incremental improvements, mindful of the acceptable level of risks, ultimately achieving the desired goal not in one step but on multiple timelines. Management's recognition of these incremental growth and revenue contributions is essential in sustaining the workforce's empowerment and motivation. Seizing on what complaints have to offer—at whatever level or whatever pace—is a classic example of seeing the glass as half full instead of half empty; notice and take advantage of the opportunity that exists rather than despair at a loss or what is problematic in a complaint.

In some cases, the process owners may perceive customer complaints as an attack on their performance. Lessons learned from the customer complaints may be used as motivation for the workforce to see the benefits of the feedback process, especially its resulting improvement opportunities. The VOC is a great source for identifying a process improvement's alignment with the customer's requirements and expectations, ultimately impacting customer satisfaction. Customer satisfaction is key in maintaining and protecting the business's health and stakeholders'/workforce's interest.

Listen to and understand the VOC.

A complaint is a "moment of truth" customer experience or perception that can alter a business partnership. Therefore, it is important for an organization to listen carefully to what a customer is saying (VOC) and leverage that, as it is a powerful tool in adding value to the system.

Discover the customers' unspoken expectations.

One benefit of customer complaints is learning customer expectations that were not previously verbalized and addressing these as part of continued satisfaction. Consider the "requirements" left unspecified by customers who thought they were part of the process by default. Consider priorities that are unique to your customer's business or workplace of which you are unaware. For instance, timely receipt of accurate information for billing purposes may be more important to a customer than receipt of on-time delivery of freight. Some customers may not necessarily be affected by freight arriving a few days late as long as there is notification; however, late and inaccurate shipment information may have a greater financial impact on the customer's process. Learning the unspoken expectations is as important as compliance to the written contract with the customer.

Ensure alignment of business direction with customer feedback.

A customer-initiated change via a customer complaint should be carefully reviewed for compatibility with the stakeholders' business direction, internal process improvement needs, and continuous improvement. While it may be another source of benefit, risks and cost of business to support this change should be analyzed to ensure mutual financial growth, compliance, and customer satisfaction. The purchase of new equipment, for instance, to expedite cycle time for a particular customer may not be practical for a product line that will be discontinued once the new business direction is kicked off in a few months.

Assess process capability's alignment with customer demands.

Assessment of process capability is another benefit of customer feedback. In some severe cases, it may be more logical from the business and the customer-relationship standpoint to discontinue or replace a process if it is no longer effective to meet the stakeholders' requirements. This may be a drastic choice and should be deployed only after considering all risks, including legal obligations. The voice of the process (i.e., process capability) should match or exceed customer demands; customer complaints on this matter are a good trigger for this initiative.

Ensure customer feedback analysis yields optimum benefits to both the customers and the organization.

Handling customer feedback can be an expensive process; gaining or losing potential business growth may rely on the effective handling of complaints. In addition, deployment of resources to assess a complaint may be a wasted effort if not properly executed. Following are some pointers in the effective handling of complaints, as complaints have a wide spectrum of severity.

Isolated complaints have many possible root causes. It is therefore imperative to create a process-screening system to easily detect if an issue is isolated or if it is a misdiagnosed case before investing resources to a full investigation. Have your screening filter verify compliance of internally controlled variables to quickly assess whether a reported issue is in fact isolated. It may include, but is not limited to, such steps as the following:

- Check historical performance or the complaint log to verify the success rate.

- Verify the error rate: Is there any evidence of a trend outside acceptable criteria?

- Check for changes in any of the typical 6Ms of the process that are within the company's control—manpower, method, measurements/metrics, material, mother nature/work environment, and machine?

It is normally easier to check these internal company-controlled variables first before evaluating variables outside the company's control. As the saying goes, "Look in the mirror before commenting about the dirt on someone's face."

Completion of such preliminary checkpoints as these will provide a foundation for asserting that internally/company-controlled process variables have been reviewed and show no apparent association with the root cause of the reported issue. This is a politically correct way of saying: *The root cause is possibly not caused by the company.*

Is this enough to satisfy the upset customer?

The answer is no. If a company has evidence that the reported incident is still within the agreed tolerance, a sufficient response to the customer to explain the situation might be: "The requirement for this process is an average of 98 percent on-time delivery within a one-month period with a standard deviation of less than 1 percent; this occurrence is still within that scope. This incident will be logged and monitored to ensure the incident remains isolated."

It should be noted that not all isolated episodes can be treated in this manner. If the impact of the isolated issue comes with high risk (e.g., plant shutdown, user safety, regulatory violation, etc.), a different response is recommended, including immediate escalation to management, development of a contingency plan, and/or taking of a preventive action.

Recurring customer complaints, regardless of severity, are a source of headache for both the customers and the company—as well as the customer perception that the company "does not care about quality." Following are some root causes of recurring complaints that should be considered during evaluation:

- Misdiagnosed problem, resulting in misaligned action
- Ineffective action plan, not confirmed to be effective
- Scope creep (i.e., customer requirements expanded beyond the agreed contract)
- Customer requirement not satisfied because it is outside the process capability of the company (e.g., customer requirement needs two-gallon volume, process can only hold one gallon).

Process capability sometimes remains a vague element of a partnership that is not always clearly defined unless the output expectations are clearly stated at the beginning of the contract with the customer. Quantified criteria help ensure visibility of the customer's expectations and the capability of the service provider (an example of a clear requirement: no recycled paper to be used in the outer box packaging of a sterile medical device).

For quick reference, a checklist of diagnostic reviews may be created to help address or prevent this scenario. During root cause analysis, it is prudent to:

- Review the agreement to ensure issues at hand are within the scope of the contract. If it is a lengthy contract, engage the help of an account manager (or similar role), who may expedite the review given his or her greater familiarity with the account's profile.

- Review process output versus issue (e.g., machine calibration tolerance versus customer requirement). If the role performing the root cause analysis is not the subject expert of the process, solicit help from other subject experts, such as the hands-on workers or engineering, to help uncover related variables.

- Review changes in the process history to see if there is any association with the issue being reported.

These are just a few of the basic verification steps that can be easily accomplished as a process of elimination to focus on other risk factors that may be associated with the resolution of the issue.

Be upfront with the customers regarding their variables contributing to the complaints.

Converting customer complaints into added value for the stakeholders is especially challenging if the root cause is a customer-controlled variable, which makes such cases sensitive. But to maintain a true long-term partnership, this variable needs to be revealed with a positive spin in place. How? Below are some proven strategies:

- **Focus on continuous improvement of the partnership.** Instead of finger pointing, focus on the benefits of resolving issues, such as cost avoidance, etc.

- **Provide a logical analysis for the problem identification or root cause analysis.** Business partners, including customers, will typically participate in the problem-solving initiatives even if the source of error is within the customer processes, if given a sound explanation of the issue.

- **Use of simple analysis methods such as trend analysis.** The parties involved (e.g., a company and its customers) are therefore not faced with finding a needle in a haystack.

- **Provide a path to the evaluation of other sources of noncompliance.** Take an open-minded approach instead of being set on one analysis. Having a rigid mindset (as opposed to being open-minded) sometimes inadvertently projects a defensive attitude that may alienate business partners or customers. Strong business partnerships and process development will further bloom using a nonbiased, open technique of problem solving. For example, discussion on the process capability versus customer requirements gap will provide visibility of roadblocks so proper options can be evaluated.

- **Focus on measurable results, making success easier to verify.** Measurable benchmarks will clarify the progress toward the expectations of the business relationship.

- **Quantify critical issues or show risk assessment.** To help neutralize a hostile environment (upset customer), this method will show severity of impact and focal point.

The aforementioned guidelines on the conversion of customer complaints into operational excellence may be kept in a centrally located documented information format for relay of knowledge and ease of retrieval. One documentation format is the failure mode and effect analysis (FMEA) format described in many quality books.

Lessons Learned

Is the customer king?

In addressing its customer's requirements, a company/business partner must consider the interests of all stakeholders. In a nut shell, if it takes millions of dollars or depleting such company resources as finances, process growth, workforce, or technology to ground zero to satisfy the customer requirements, the risk must be carefully evaluated by management to ensure the actions taken are commensurate with the risk. Taking no action or executing a poor root cause analysis are only invitations for reoccurrence of the problem. At the very least, such occurrences should be acknowledged and recorded.

Note: There are exceptions to this philosophy, such as, but not limited to, resource-rich, brand-name companies geared to satisfy customers at all cost, since there is a guaranteed revenue associated with the product or service provided by the company. These companies are willing to take the financial risks involved, as there is probably more to lose in certain situations if the opportunity/risk is ignored (e.g., strong foreign competition for lower price).

If a customer extends the service requirement (scope creep) through complaint after the agreement approval, what is the best way to respond to this feedback?

It is not uncommon to receive complaints (e.g., superficial requirements that are vague) that are beyond the agreed-upon process capability or level of service to be provided. This is particularly common if the acceptance criteria of a commodity or service are not clearly defined upfront and/or are subject to broad interpretation (e.g., such concerns as packaging damage, cosmetic appearance, etc.).

One way to begin addressing the feedback is to review the contract agreement; if the information is still vague and does not offer a clear line on the acceptance criteria, check the customer feedback or complaint log. If there are no similar complaints from similar customers using the same process, it may be isolated to a particular customer (scope creep) or a customer requirement was not fully assessed during contract review. Such an action may need more time to resolve; thus, it is best to inform the customer of the preliminary finding immediately, so the customer has reasonable expectations and is not in a long waiting mode. In some cases, if the complaint is truly isolated and is not part of a repeating pattern, process-performance data may be used to show the inherent process variation. Regardless of the cause (isolated or due to a special cause), the provider needs to respond to the customer.

If the complaint reported to the company is not the company's fault, should a customer-mandated corrective action form be completed?

Some customer complaints are tied to a financial fine or scorecard that will "blemish" the company on the record. In some cases, mandated reports go through websites that automatically issue a negative score to the company.

One course of action is to first contact the customer issuing the complaint by letter or email so it's recorded and follow up with a phone call to explain that the root cause analysis clearly showed the complaint is not applicable to the company. Customers will likely understand the situation if given enough information in writing during the initial contact and will hopefully retract the corrective-action request. A site visit (if practical and depending on the customer account) may also be beneficial to show due diligence and protect the long-term business relationship with the customer.

Retaining the customer base through this escalation step is one of the training modules that needs to be part of the QMS, as it can easily get off tangent if not contained properly.

Customer complaints come in many forms; the organization must be ready to handle challenging situations outside the typical format to ensure proper assessment of the VOC. For example, how do you handle a rude customer who curses at people during conference calls?

A business relationship should presume mutual respect of the parties involved. The customer does not have the right to treat its providers below the level of expected human courtesy in the business world.

One diplomatic way of addressing such poor behavior is to state something like, "Customer *x*, we appreciate your concern over this issue, and we are willing to work with you to resolve the problem; we can make this meeting more productive if we stay focused on the subject." Most decent people will get the clue that cursing is not an acceptable way of doing business with the company. However, if the rudeness and cursing continue, the meeting member may add, "We will stop this meeting and will reschedule it once you are ready to discuss our business issue." This technique should be conveyed to the rest of the company's customer support team to make it visible in a firm but polite way that the company does not tolerate inhumane treatment of the company's employees.

This customer-service technique should be part of the organization's employee-customer relationship training (e.g., guidelines on how to deal with difficult people) to further empower the workforce and continue a compliant and strong QMS program.

Auditor's Perspective

A QMS designer may have installed the critical-to-quality elements necessary to gain positive customer feedback with the best intentions of meeting the standard governing the QMS, as well as the stakeholders' interest; however, the QMS may still fail the auditor's perspective. How can this happen? As discussed earlier, the QMS is a living document and may have passed an auditor's assessment in the past, but changes with negative impact on the QMS may have occurred after that last audit.

For instance, some customers with a long-term relationship with a company may have developed certain unwritten expectations that are understood and fulfilled by the company contact who is cementing the long-term successful business relationship (e.g., face-to-face site visit every quarter to discuss project status or resolve customer questions preventing complaints). However, even a typical change in any company such as a "changing of the guards" situation (e.g., retirement of a key employee) may potentially have a negative impact on the QMS balance or customer satisfaction if the change's risk is not carefully assessed. In this scenario, the unwritten customer expectation could pose a risk of customer dissatisfaction, increase in customer complaints, or loss of business if these expectations are not properly relayed to the replacement employee. This situation will create further risk if there is no structured change control or knowledge management program (e.g., cross-training, process documentation, etc.) to prevent gaps when a system disruption occurs such as the departure of key personnel or SME.

This is not only an operational risk to the company but also a potential regulatory compliance risk if the change fails the auditor's perspective.

How can an auditor detect this internal issue? One common tool used by the auditor to detect changes and effectiveness is the verification of a change documentation or simply asking the question, "What recent changes have occurred within the last x number of months?" and asking for some examples. This will give the auditor a starting platform to verify the effectiveness of the change and its impact on the system. Failure to properly validate the change effectiveness will be revealed in the records (such as trending of complaints after a personnel change). Once the discrepancy is exposed, the auditor's perspective and confidence with the system will dramatically change.

Identification of Risks and Improvement Opportunities—Discovering Hidden Factories and Using the Process Grid Walk

■──■

Risk is an element that is present in all phases of any business. The process-risk interrelationship and risk-mitigation methods should be documented, verified, and measured to ensure visibility, accountability, and performance measurement. Systems that are process-oriented and include risk mitigation have a higher probability of success than a system without these mechanisms. Risk-mitigation success factors include the identification of risks and the integration of the risk-prevention initiatives or contingency plans in the QMS. There are many methods to accomplish the discovery of risks, many of which can often be disguised as part of a "hidden factory" (that is, not easily visible in the system). These methods include auditing beyond compliance, a performance metrics review program, or a gap analysis, as depicted in Figure 4.1.

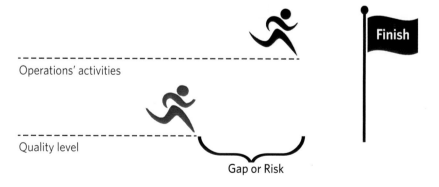

Operations' activities

Quality level

Gap or Risk

Figure 4.1 Pictorial depiction of gap or risk.

(Smith 2012b)

Risk is an unavoidable element with different levels of severity present in all phases of any system. Risk is sometimes not easily visible, as it may be a byproduct of an action or a decision (e.g., investing in a product line that is short-lived due to a competitor's capture of the market via a cheaper foreign market source). Once the organization identifies its core processes that are susceptible to risks, the next step is to choose a strategy to address the risks with the greatest impact on the business goal/s (e.g., adding a new product line or service to pursue market expansion). One method of identifying hidden factories is through the implementation of auditing beyond compliance, as depicted in Figure 4.2.

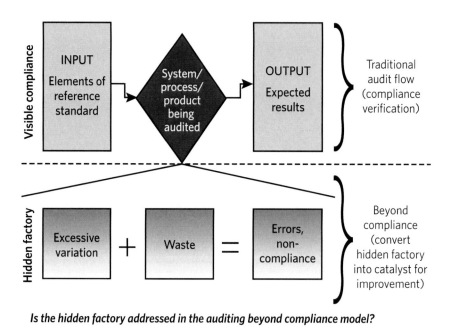

Is the hidden factory addressed in the auditing beyond compliance model?

Figure 4.2 Discovery of risks disguised as a "hidden factory" through auditing beyond compliance.[3]

(ASQ Audit Division 2016)

---

[3] The auditing beyond compliance auditing method is further discussed in Chapter 9 of this book.

The auditing beyond compliance model in Figure 4.2 provides visibility of the process-risk interrelationship. The following are critical steps in the detection of risks:

- Recognize the signs of risk and know a particular risk's real name (e.g., financial risk).

- Measure. Do data mining to quantify severity.

- Find out its hiding place and convert the risk into an improvement. Identify the processes that are impacted; follow the errors, gaps, or roadblocks expressed by the process owners.

These variables are shown in Figure 4.3.

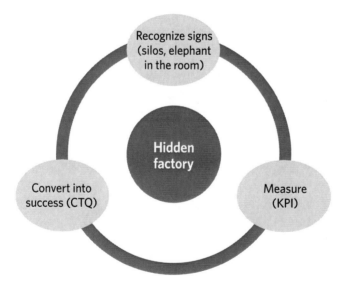

Figure 4.3 Guidelines: How to detect and measure risks. Note: Critical-to-quality (CTQ) and key performance indicators (KPI); elephant in the room is an element being ignored; silo means information blocked from flowing.

(Smith 2014)

Are risk discussions only applicable to the executives with the authority to make business decisions? Absolutely not! Management's decision is also impacted by variables considered in management review, such as the effectiveness of actions taken to address risk and opportunities.[4] In short, input for risk mitigation may come from other sources, such as internal processes or business partners' input or complaints.

Process Grid Walk

This section will share a tool designed by the author, implemented and validated through the scrutinizing of both internal and external audits, including third-party auditors: The process grid walk (PGW) is a proven and time-tested model that is a simple but effective quality tool in the identification, mitigation, and resolution of risks—improvement opportunities—within a system. This is part of the auditing beyond compliance concept.[5]

The PGW has been cited as a best practice in the logistics industry in one of the validation audit reports issued by the U.S. Customs and Border Protection (CBP). This commendation was reported during the Customs Trade Partnership Against Terrorism (C-TPAT) certification, a security certification of ProTrans, a third-party logistics (3PL) company. This tool has been implemented by the author (Janet Smith) for more than 25 years in companies under various regulatory governances—medical device manufacturing under FDA regulation, commercial/automotive companies under ISO/TS standards—with successful results.

PGW is an incremental verification and measurement of performance concept in the vein of *eat the elephant one bite at a time* (otherwise, it is an overwhelming task). This is just a metaphor to give an overview of the concept, not a promotion of eating an elephant! Start by defining the core processes (e.g., process, business unit, product line, etc.) one bite at a time.

PGW should not be confused with a Gemba Walk. A Gemba Walk is a lean tool that refers to walking through the area where a process is located, typically performed by different levels of management, to get exposure and knowledge of the processes/system.

---

[4] ISO 9001:2015, 9.3.2.e
[5] Janet Smith, *Auditing Beyond Compliance* (Milwaukee: Quality Press, 2012).

Key components of the PGW (see Figure 4.4):

- PGW is dynamic, representing the voice of the process through the participation of the process owners.

- PGW documents and monitors actions.

- PGW is performed by the subject experts or process owners.

- PGW becomes part of the internal audit input.

- PGW is a self-audit with bias removed through the involvement and follow-up of an independent facilitator (e.g., quality department).

- PGW methodology and results have been accepted/approved by several external/certification audits including the ISO standard.

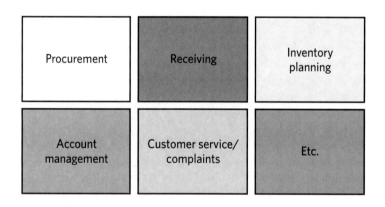

Figure 4.4 Process grid walk—identify core processes. Note: Drill down; each core process may be further broken down into sub-cores.

In essence, PGW is an incremental evaluation of processes similar to an archeological dig's grid analysis of a site under review. Instead of the archeologists, the process owners are the subject experts participating in the review of the process under study. PGWs performed by the subject experts and process owners are likely to detect hidden factories (hidden anomalies) that are not easily detected during traditional audits. Process owners have intimate knowledge or experience with the hidden factories, as most of these incongruities are part of their day-to-day pains and roadblocks, yet they do not surface when an auditor is on hand. Examples of some such pains and roadblocks are outlined in Table 4.1.

Hidden factories— scenarios	Possible causes
Mediocre performance hidden by self-endorsement	Employee promotion program based on a "firework show" instead of a structured merit program. A firework show means an initiative that is impressive at first glance but not sustainable, such as fireworks. **Example:** An employee with low qualifications but a strong ability to self-endorse may influence the promotion process. **Countermeasure:** Company/management should encourage process or project metrics for accountability.
Unqualified staff or area leader	Qualifications for a role not clearly identified, structured, or followed. **Example:** It is always commendable to see employees achieve professional certifications (such as a project management certificate) as part of personal growth. Industry certifications that are achieved through the study of test materials are an added value to a role. However, certifications should not be taken as the sole replacement of education, background discipline, or experience if these elements are required. If requirements are bypassed, this action will not only have a negative impact on the company, but it will also affect the workforce morale. The employee in this category will likely be frustrated (underqualified) and may create reasons to apply to or move on from role to role within the company to cover incompetence—it is not unusual for an employee of this nature to use the "sympathy card" of not "being happy anymore" in his or her existing department. This is an example of the Peter Paul Principle—not a good cycle in a lean business. The Peter Paul Principle means the resource (Paul) moving to another role will be replaced by taking another resource (Peter) to cover for the incompetence of another (Paul).

Table 4.1 Hidden factories seen by PGWs.   *(continued)*

Hidden factories— scenarios	Possible causes
Unqualified staff or area leader	There is an exception to this rule: If the industry certification is the sole requirement for the role and/or the employee excels over the other qualified candidates, then it is an acceptable criterium. **Countermeasure:** Companies are encouraged to clearly identify requirements for the job functions to avoid the Peter Paul Principle and focus on promotion by merits. Performance metrics or feedback from previous managers are useful input for the assessment process and should be part of the employee evaluation.
Monkey see, monkey do	Unclear organizational policies may be a breeding ground for abuse by employees who lack self-discipline and are insensitive to coworkers. **Examples:** • Late arrival to work or meetings • Frequent/daily prolonged closed office doors to perform personal tasks (obvious to staff and coworkers) • Constant use of cell phones on nonemergency personal level during meetings **Countermeasure:** Companies are encouraged to clearly identify requirements for the job functions. For example, identify and enforce the use of allocated sanctuary rooms to perform personal tasks rather than using the office meant for business transactions.

Table 4.1 Hidden factories seen by PGWs.

The PGW is a versatile tool that uses existing subject expert resources with optimum positive impact on risk management. See an overview of the concept presented in Figure 4.5.

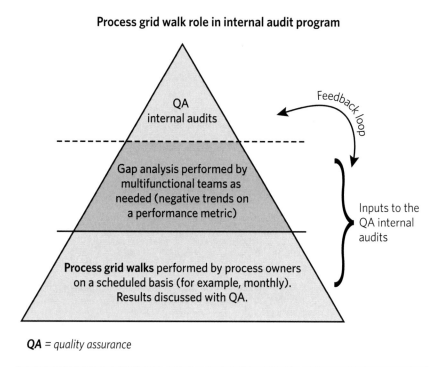

Process grid walk role in internal audit program

QA = *quality assurance*

Figure 4.5 Overview of the PGW model—a tool to help detect risks. Note: Process grid walks and identification of gaps in the process are likely to uncover associated risks.

Figure 4.6 shows an example of a PGW log. The starfish and turtles are icons assigned to show the status of the PGW. A starfish is used for on-time submission and a turtle is used for late or no submission.

To: Management Review Team Cc: Operations **Monthly Process Grid Walks Report** **Month XX Year XX**		
Monthly process grid walk (Grid scope description on file)	**Process grid walk report (completed and discussed with QA per schedule)** **Note: Complete report on file in x location.**	**Status Icon**  On-time submission  Late or no submission
Grid 1: Shipping Dept. Reported by Chet Smith, Facility Manager—Indiana location	Completed	
Grid 2: Receiving Dept. Reported by Bryan Santos, Area Manager—California location	Completed	
Grid 3: Staging Dept. Reported by John Jones, Area Manager—Florida location	No submission	

Figure 4.6 Example of PGW log.

(Smith 2019)

The PGW initiative was once explained by the author to a business partner as part of the supply chain development program. The business partner commented: "Process grid walk is just a self-audit. It is not a new method; anyone can do that. I do that every day by walking around the plant to ensure everything is in place." That assertion may be true, but his activity does not capture the scope or the optimum benefit of the PGW model. The following elements make the PGW different from *walking around the plant to ensure everything is in place*:

- Structured activity is combined with a checklist of core processes for verifying performance beyond compliance, which includes risks present in the processes under evaluation. The checklist is specific to the grid under review.

- Core processes and subprocesses are divided as "grids" to facilitate incremental evaluation of the system—one grid per PGW cycle (eating the elephant one bite at a time)—and verified throughout the year. Prioritization of the grids is at the process owner's discretion.

- A scheduled frequency (e.g., monthly) ensures all identified core grids are verified.

- PGW is performed by existing subject experts or process owners as an incremental self-audit with QA intervention and follow-up to remove bias (i.e., input to the QA internal audit program).

- Results are documented and tracked by QA in a simple log for easy follow-up of actions' completion.

- Open items are assigned with deadlines and distributed to process owners and area management for visibility.

- QA is involved in helping the process owners pursue the actions required. There is a provision in the checklist that if nonconformances are purposely not reported during the PGW, then these items will be counted against the process owners. One motivator for the process owners to disclose potential nonconformances and challenges is QA's commitment to helping the process owners escalate their roadblocks to the next level.

- The PGW summaries/actions are input to the QA internal audits as an added tool in auditing beyond compliance.

A PGW checklist will vary depending on the grid or process under evaluation. It may be as short as 15 minutes or as long as one hour, depending on the complexity of the grid being evaluated.

This tool can be easily implemented with no additional resources, just a different mentality from *walking around the plant to ensure everything is in place*. Some of the elements involved in the PGW are shown in Figure 4.7.

Process grid walk role—organization vision and quality program

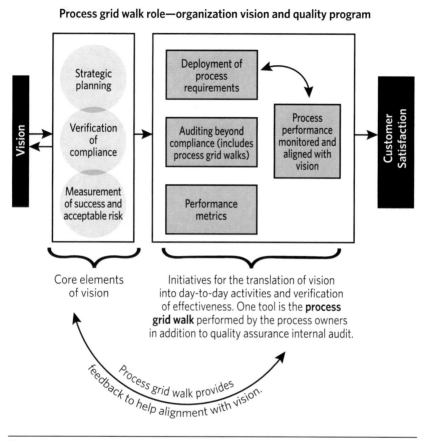

Figure 4.7 Process grid walk overview.

(Smith 2019)

Process Grid Walk Scenarios

Let's look at two examples to see the PGW in action. These examples reflect the effectiveness of the PGW as a tool for risk mitigation and initiating continuous improvement.

Scenario 1

A team of process owners chose to evaluate the freight pickup/delivery trend for that month's scheduled PGW. The sampled records showed the beginning of a late-delivery trend for a certain product line. Although there was no customer complaint, the process owner selected the evaluation of this grid to identify any improvement opportunity.

Results of the PGW: It was discovered that the supplier was slowly converting the freight packaging into a modified configuration without notification, thus impacting the trailer pickup of freight (that is, dimensions of the new configuration did not fit the pickup trailer to transport the freight). Based on this discovery, other questions were listed to fine-tune the root cause analysis:

- Is there a packaging specification maintained under controlled documentation to prevent unauthorized changes?

- Is there a change control program that could have prevented the impact of this packaging change? If so, are the process owners aware of the policy?

- Are the above documented?

This open discussion via the PGW will increase the supplier's awareness on accountability and compliance with requirements. The next PGW cycle should focus on the follow-up on progress of the actions.

These findings were escalated to the proper teams for resolution, including a provision for the supplier's change approval. The PGW is a simple tool for identifying such improvement opportunities.

Scenario 2

Company A issued a complaint against the manufacturer, requiring a corrective action plan. The manufacturer has strong evidence that the error occurred due to Company A's specification change without notifying the manufacturer. The manufacturer, just like other organizations under the same scenario, was reluctant to respond to the web-based complaint, as Company A's online complaint system automatically gives a negative score to the business partners issued with a complaint. Corrective action plans are good tools for documenting the problem statement, root cause, and any containment and other actions needed to minimize or prevent reoccurrence.[6] In some cases, such as this example, a documentation on why a corrective action plan may not be applicable via a letter, telephone call, or site visit

---

[6] Janet B. Smith, "Rapid Response: The Right Way to Address Customer Complaints." *Quality Progress* (July 2010).

should be considered as a discussion point with the customer. Ignoring the online request for a corrective action plan from the customer will not solve the issue and may result in a worse situation—lost business.

Scenario 3

Customer A has issued numerous complaints to its logistics service company regarding freight damages at the receiving point. The logistics company's director of quality then coordinated an investigation that entailed a thorough review of the freight handling, starting from the point of pickup at the customer's supplier to handling at the logistics company's consolidation point. The study included the review of the common 6Ms of the process (listed below) at the touch points (pickup from supplier, consolidation of freight, and shipment):

- **M**aterial associated with the freight, such as supplier packaging
- **M**anpower, such as staff training on handling
- **M**ethod of handling
- **M**achines involved in the handling of freight, such as forklifts
- **M**other nature/work environment
- **M**easurement of processes

From this scenario, it was concluded that the customer's supplier changed the packaging material configuration of the freight (without notifying the customer), triggering the damages during transportation. This finding highlighted the added value of the logistics company's evaluation, which helped resolve the customer issue. The PGW of the 6Ms as part of the continuing process evaluations will benefit the improvement program.

Lessons Learned

Mitigation of risks can be viewed as opportunities for continuous improvement. Identification of risks does not have to be a long-haul gap analysis or audit; it can be a simplified task and focused on the likely variables associated with the risk. One tool discussed in this chapter, the PGW, can be easily deployed as a streamlined evaluation tool by subject experts or process owners.

How are risks identified?

One method of identifying the risk associated with a process or department is to first identify management's expectations from that department or process as commonly depicted in metrics. For example, a process expected to complete a certain cycle time to produce a certain volume of output can use these parameters to start identifying risks or roadblocks if expectations are not consistently met. This analysis will help identify first the risk and then the mitigation plan.

What are some common methods for mitigating risks and converting them to improvement opportunities?

Before a mitigation plan can be formulated, one must understand the risk. In the example above, the risk identified was a resource shortage during certain days or seasons. Once risk is understood, options to mitigate can be generated, and the most logical, efficient, or effective one can be chosen. In this example, could subcontracting during that risky period of resource shortage be the most logical choice, or should there be a change in planning and scheduling of shipments? The answer will depend on the shareholders' requirements.

What motivates the process owners/subject experts to display their "dirty laundry" during the PGW reporting?

The process owners are given an "immunity" guarantee that no consequences will occur if they supply an honest list of issues that were uncovered. QA or a designated team will help do the root cause analysis or help follow up with management to mitigate the discovered roadblocks. However, if there is proof that anomalies were uncovered and intentionally hidden during the QA (or designate) sampling, consequences will occur (such as a write-up). The above motivator helped convert the process owners' apprehension to appreciation and acknowledgment from peers and management.

What is the significance of the starfish and turtle icons in the PGW report log?

Instead of a lengthy report on the status of the PGW, it is simpler to use a starfish or turtle icon to identify completion status for easy visibility by management and process owners. It is an impressive observation of human nature's pride of work—no one wants a turtle.

Why should a company use the PGW initiative mentioned in this chapter?

- PGW involves participation and buy-in of process owners and management.

- PGW results (discoveries of wastes/hidden factories) are beneficial inputs in an internal audit program, where findings can be followed up on and closed.

- PGW has been audited and accepted as part of the internal audit program by external auditors such as ISO auditors and C-TPAT auditors.

- It was quoted as one of the best practices in an internal audit report by a C-TPAT auditor in a 2017 validation of ProTrans's C-TPAT certification.

Auditor's Perspective

This chapter discussed the different methods of identifying and mitigating risks focusing on the QMS designers' and stakeholders' perspectives. Regardless of the meticulous methods laid out to address the risks and opportunities, there is always a chance certain elements may have been inadvertently omitted and may likely be discovered first by the auditor's eagle eyes. The auditor's discovery can include a new risk or an existing identified risk with a new level of severity per the auditor's perspective. This discovery should not trigger a panic mode for the company if the QMS has a path of containment or immediate mitigation process until the risk discovery can be fully assessed and resolved. Arguing or justifying the finding with the auditor is the least effective way of addressing the issue. Showing the auditor a structured system to deal with such a discovery for further analysis and resolution is the critical element that will have more impact on the auditor's perspective on the QMS's stability and readiness to handle unexpected situations with possible impact on the system.

One model for a structured system may involve assigning different teams or subject experts to assess the different levels of risks on a periodic basis or to assess risks based on indicators such as process changes, market shifts, etc. occurring in the system (whether product, system, or process related). The auditor's perspective should be considered a free improvement input for the continuing assessment of the QMS.

5

An Effective and Efficient Documentation System to Support a QMS and Satisfy an Auditor

There is no one rule for satisfying the document control requirements of all stakeholders, regardless of the quality standard governing the business. The continuing success of any quality system depends on quality pillars, including an effective document control program. In most cases, quality standards, such as the ISO standard, do not specify how the document control requirements can be met, as this is dependent on the companies' business variables.

Procedure or report writing guidelines are readily available online and in many books; however, it is far less common to easily locate strategies on mitigating document control downfalls. The same goes for the implementation of lean solutions for a documentation system that are based on actual experience and validation from an independent source, whether that's acceptance by a customer or an external audit. That is the goal of this section: to share lessons learned from developing and implementing document systems for maintaining effective quality systems.

Figure 5.1 depicts a typical documentation flow.

Common Pitfalls and Lean Solutions

Example 1: Documented instructions for multiple processes

Common pitfalls: Complex and interrelated processes are sometimes documented under one document for optimization purpose. Routine pitfalls in this method include:

- Confusion and user error from lengthy verbiage.

- Cumbersome change management. If there is a change in one of the processes listed under one document, the entire document needs

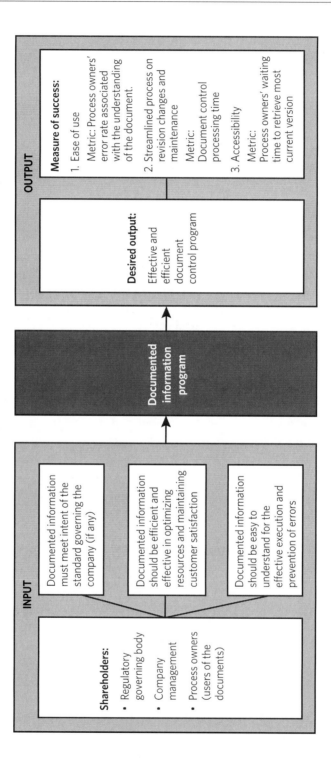

Figure 5.1 Typical documentation model.

(Smith 2012c)

to be modified. Even with the presence of sophisticated electronic systems, a simple change may require resubmission to regulatory agencies (e.g., FDA product submission); therefore, it is best to start with a streamlined documentation.

- Key subprocesses that may remain hidden within too much information

Example of a lean solution: Break down main or core processes and identify the sub-elements under each core process serving as a document map; each core process may be documented separately and cross-referenced for easy tracking. Using the sample format in Figure 5.2 will help remove the noise (unnecessary details) in the process, making the hidden factories more visible.

There are many software packages available to help in this simplification depending on an organization's budget and technology availability. Regardless of what is used, it is imperative that the document breakdown and mapping are understood by the process owners, as they form the foundation of a good documentation.

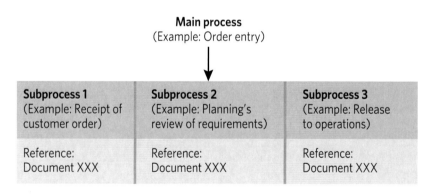

Figure 5.2 Sample document format.

Consider, for demonstration, that Department A has five core processes, and the engineering manager is proposing to document these five interrelated processes in one document for simplicity's sake. A quality director may point out that the simplicity benefit mentioned by the engineering manager is valid, but also that there are risks/wastes involved in putting the five separate processes in one document:

- A simple change in one of the processes will put the entire document under revision, even if the other four processes have no changes (waste: waiting time).

- Similarly, if the five processes are in one document, changes to any one process may require a lengthy FDA approval despite only one process being changed. It is easier and faster to clarify the isolated process being changed as opposed to when it is combined in documentation with four other processes.

Recommended format: To achieve the engineering manager's objective, document each process separately, but keep the five documents together in one "folder" like a manual. The document control gatekeeper can create an electronic folder containing the five core processes as subsidiary items, as shown in Figure 5.3. By clustering the documents in this way, it remains clear where the change occurred.

Example 2: Creation of a process flowchart

A process flowchart is one format for documenting the process steps, in lieu of or in parallel with written documentation, to provide reference or guidelines to the process owner.

Common pitfalls of a process flowchart:

- Process owners are not defined, as a typical flowchart just shows the sequence of steps.

- Critical-to-quality (CTQ) measures of success are not clarified to help guide process owners in measurement of performance.

Example of a lean solution: Criteria or measures of success must be clear and, if possible, quantifiable, to eliminate subjective interpretation. A visual model, rather than a wordy document, may be used, as depicted in Table 5.1. This template shows not only the sequential steps of the process but also the process owner of the steps and the CTQ measures. An enhanced flowchart like this one can be created to document a range of processes, whether very simple or complex. It is easy to implement and understand. The details needed to create such a chart may require the input of a typical multifunctional team involved in the documentation of a process (example input of the engineering department for raw material specifications). This documentation technique should not require added resources; it is just a different documentation format.

The five separate subprocesses are numbered as subsidiary of the core process identifier. Below is an example of numbering hierarchy for this model of documentation:

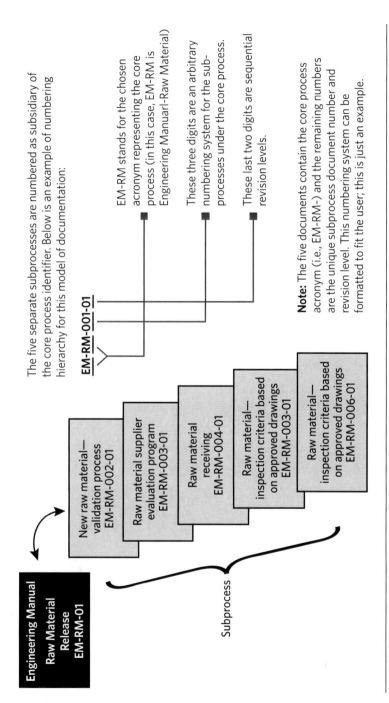

EM-RM-001-01

■ EM-RM stands for the chosen acronym representing the core process (in this case, EM-RM is Engineering Manuarl-Raw Material)

■ These three digits are an arbitrary numbering system for the sub-processes under the core process.

■ These last two digits are sequential revision levels.

Note: The five documents contain the core process acronym (i.e., EM-RM-) and the remaining numbers are the unique subprocess document number and revision level. This numbering system can be formatted to fit the user; this is just an example.

Engineering Manual
Raw Material
Release
EM-RM-01

New raw material—
validation process
EM-RM-002-01

Raw material supplier
evaluation program
EM-RM-003-01

Raw material
receiving
EM-RM-004-01

Raw material—
inspection criteria based
on approved drawings
EM-RM-003-01

Raw material—
inspection criteria based
on approved drawings
EM-RM-006-01

Subprocess

Figure 5.3 Clustering of related documents.

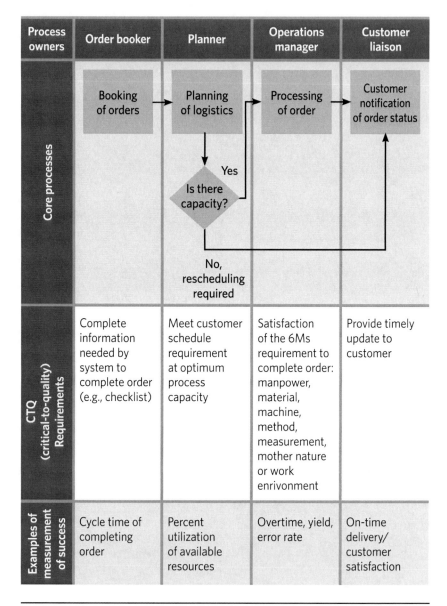

Process owners	Order booker	Planner	Operations manager	Customer liaison
Core processes	Booking of orders	Planning of logistics	Processing of order	Customer notification of order status
CTQ (critical-to-quality) Requirements	Complete information needed by system to complete order (e.g., checklist)	Meet customer schedule requirement at optimum process capacity	Satisfaction of the 6Ms requirement to complete order: manpower, material, machine, method, measurement, mother nature or work enrivonment	Provide timely update to customer
Examples of measurement of success	Cycle time of completing order	Percent utilization of available resources	Overtime, yield, error rate	On-time delivery/ customer satisfaction

Table 5.1 Sample document format for a process flowchart. Such documentation also increases the visibility of the process requirements and performance measurement (i.e., CTQ measures). This format may be used in lieu of a wordy procedure. The document is not only an instruction guideline but may also be used as a template for recording the process scorecard.

(Document concept/format from Smith 2012a)

Example 3: Creation of survey form

Common pitfall: Rigid and lengthy quality questionnaires are returned at low rates. In business, time is money; a customer may view completing a lengthy survey for a business partner's internal compliance as "waste" and not prioritize it.

Example of a lean solution: The KISS method is the crux of the solution, i.e., *keep it short and simple.* Provide flexible options, including offering an alternative to completing a survey, such as submitting a copy of the company's certificate (such as ISO, etc.).

Sample document format: Put a provision on top of your survey form such as: "Are you currently certified to quality standard x? (obviously, state the standard under survey, e.g., ISO). If yes, send a copy of the recent certificate, and sign and date the bottom of the survey page. There is no need to complete the survey."

Example 4: Streamlining of documents, or minimizing non-added value and waste embedded within documentation

Common pitfall: Some organizations do not have dedicated work instruction writers, meaning document control happens in a vast array of formats and styles as interpreted by the subject matter experts. In some cases, the instructions are cumbersome, with inefficient information flow that can later cause user confusion and error. What can the person handling document control do if time and resource restrictions prevent a fine-tune editing of these documents?

Example of a lean solution: Documented information may be formatted in many ways with the goal of making it user friendly. One simple way is shown in Table 5.2—using a matrix instead of abundant text to describe the intent of the document, measurement of success, and escalation if goals are not met. The area manager of the process can provide such details to ensure accuracy and ownership. This information may then be verified during PGWs, as described in Chapter 4.

Core processes	Metrics	Goal	Escalation path if below goal
Order entry	Monthly percent order completion versus customer requirement	98–100%	Submit a 5 Whys for root cause analysis and action plan; include review in management review documentation of trend.
Processing/ delivery	Monthly on-time delivery of shipments	98–100%	

Table 5.2 Sample documentation of core processes and metrics.

Example 5: Documentation of management review

Common pitfall: Some companies document the management review element once a year, producing a huge compilation of data based on the highlights of the year covering the management review inputs and outputs. The common approach becomes something of an historic timeline that is static and may not necessarily trigger actions on improvement.

Example of a lean solution: The incremental documentation of management review is more robust than a one-time management meeting at the end of the year, providing timely feedback on the status or performance of the company and more opportunities for addressing the gaps.

An easier and more manageable method of documentation is the creation of a checklist itemizing the required elements to be verified during a management review (e.g., inputs and outputs required by the ISO standard). By documenting activities or initiatives related to each element throughout the year as evidence, the management review will be transformed into a more dynamic and living document rather than a history post of events, as when done only at the end of the year. This incremental documentation method will be effective if there are process owners assigned to complete this task on a scheduled, standard basis.

Sample document format: Using some of the input/output requirements of management review under ISO 9001:2015 as an example, following is a checklist format that may be completed by the designated process owner for submission to QA or other designated role:

Element	Jan.	Feb.	Mar.	Etc.	Dec.
Status of actions from previous management	Completed. See Report xx/ located in zz				
Changes in external and internal issues relevant to the quality management system		Discussed in operations meeting. See Report yy/ located in zz			
Customer feedback			Reviewed trend from xx-to-xx		Second review of trend to cover annual data—Report xx
Etc.					

Table 5.3 Annual management incremental review—year xx.

A few words of caution:

Each report referenced in the management review form listed in Table 5.3 should:

- Be easy to retrieve
- Be in a simplified format
- Contain a simple summary, including a statement on the effectiveness of the system
- Provide an action plan with owner/timeline that should be noted if there are gaps

Lessons Learned

In considering the latest available technology options for improving a documentation program, do not lose focus on the basic elements that will have the greatest impact on compliance, customer improvement, and customer satisfaction. Regardless of the technology, it is still vital to understand process mapping alignment with the process capability and customer requirements as guidelines in designing an effective and efficient document control program.

Should intricate details be included in the process flowchart? It is at the discretion of the company/process owners to define the level of details needed in any flowchart. In general, some steps may be omitted from the main process flowchart, especially if there are other relevant reference documents. Example: Calibration of a piece of equipment may be detailed in the calibration procedures, but these details are not included in the flowchart of a process (for example, a receiving flowchart may cite the inspection of dimensions using a caliper, but the caliper's calibration steps are not included in the flowchart).

Auditor's Perspective

Document control is one of the most visible and verifiable elements of the QMS. Elements of document control may vary, depending on the standard or customer requirements associated with the QMS. This book cannot emphasize enough the importance of documentation regardless of the company business and customer base. Document control should not only support the QMS designer and company stakeholders, but it should also provide the evidence necessary to satisfy the auditor's perspective.

The auditor's perspective is not limited to the presence of documents or records to be reviewed during an audit; the auditor also reviews the integrity and relevance of these documents in ensuring compliance and customer satisfaction. The auditor's focus on document control includes, but is not limited to, simplicity (keeping it short and simple), robustness, ease of deployment, and whether it has been embraced by the workforce.

A project management software, for example, may be easy for the project department in tracking project status, since it is the department's main tool and primary duty; however, if other sectors of the business, including the customers, deem this tool as complicated, causing delayed document updating, then it is an ineffective tool. This observation can be noted through the auditor's sampling of visible success indicators such as timeliness and cycle time of tool update and process owners' feedback. The auditor may conclude that it is an ineffective document control aid and may cite the situation as an improvement opportunity. Another weakness of document control that may be more obvious to the auditor is the overdoing of documentation to suggest an impressive creation but that actually causes difficulty for the users. As an example, a simple flowchart may be better in showing and reviewing core processes' flow than a long, complicated flowchart that includes non-value-added or non-critical steps. Such a situation may not rise to the level of an auditing discrepancy unless it causes delays in updating the document due to its complexity; complex documents may actually contribute to internal noncompliance if any of those non-value-added or non-critical steps are not updated to match actual tasks. Keep documents simple and easy to understand...and easy to update.

6

QMS Operational Compliance and Excellence Within Processes

One critical factor in achieving consistent customer and stakeholder satisfaction comes from the operational compliance and excellence that is built in the process. However, some companies face many challenges to accomplishing a consistent level of the desired performance if customer expectations exceed the company's capability level, what's commonly known as a process gap. Take, for example, a company that has a process performance output of +/– 20 percent thickness tolerance, with a customer that has an acceptable thickness level of +/– 15 percent. Since the customer expectation is tighter than the process performance level (i.e., a gap), the output will likely result in some unacceptable products that will either be rejected or sorted for rework (i.e., the use of brute force, which means the use of unnecessary efforts to achieve a goal) to maintain specification.

Early detection of these gaps will prevent or lessen the risks' impact on the stakeholders; however, capability gaps exist in many forms and may be hidden in some phases of business operations, making them difficult to spot and mitigate. Not all gaps are permanent; some gaps may be easily resolved through continuous improvement initiatives (e.g., replacing an old machine with newer technology to meet customer product tolerance).

Management support is critical in driving continuous improvement initiatives in response to such issues as the one discussed previously. Let's look at a couple real quotes reflecting true management commitment, buy-in, in customer satisfaction and continuous improvement programs.

"The process needs to identify the required inputs, but the solution is not the process....[I]t is the system that needs to require the process to be completed effectively during the normal workflow as shipments move through the network and system simultaneously. Expecting that the process and/or flowchart will fix this is outdated in our complex environment. The business has too many moving parts, the speed in which we operate requires quick, quality, and sustainable resolutions to get things corrected across multiple teams.

As the required inputs or gaps in the process are identified, we need to determine where we can incorporate these variables into the teams' and the system workflow."

— Shawn Masters, Chief Commercial Officer
ProTrans (3PL/Logistics Company), Indianapolis, IN

"Accomplishing goals using brute force is a waste of resources. It means a company exerted a lot of unnecessary efforts to get the task done. The process should be streamlined, efficient, and repeatable."

— Lisa Doerner, Chief Financial Officer
ProTrans (3PL/Logistics Company), Indianapolis, IN

Next is a real quote from a regulatory agent, an external government auditor focused on security, depicting the importance of commitment to operational compliance and excellence within a process.

"Managers all have their own analytical perception and interpretation of the same facts as presented. Companies that move managers to evaluate other areas of supply chain security have resulted in positive results in identifying areas for improvement. The objective of the exercise is to protect your company and have the ability to provide documentation and evidence of a process or procedure that proves the breach did not occur within your facility.

Note: Chart the movement of your cargo and understand your logistics providers' processes. Know if your cargo is being subcontracted to the lowest bidder."

— Ricardo Villarreal, Supply Chain Security Specialist
C-TPAT Field Office, U.S. Customs and Border Protection

To maintain satisfaction, compliance, and operational excellence, customer requirements or changes need to be continually communicated to the system for their ongoing alignment with the operational processes. Figure 6.1 is a model depicting a closed-loop feedback that can help in achieving operational compliance and excellence within a process. This model may be used as a template for verifying the effectiveness of a system's alignment of customer requirements against process capability.

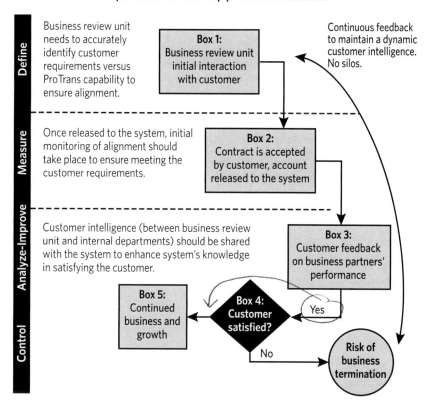

Figure 6.1 Sample DMAIC path to help achieve operational compliance and excellence within a process.

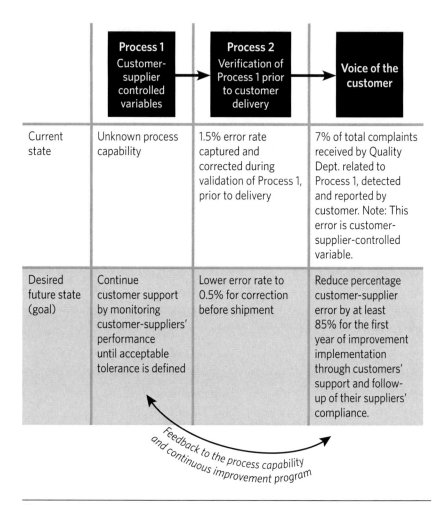

	Process 1 Customer-supplier controlled variables	Process 2 Verification of Process 1 prior to customer delivery	Voice of the customer
Current state	Unknown process capability	1.5% error rate captured and corrected during validation of Process 1, prior to delivery	7% of total complaints received by Quality Dept. related to Process 1, detected and reported by customer. Note: This error is customer-supplier-controlled variable.
Desired future state (goal)	Continue customer support by monitoring customer-suppliers' performance until acceptable tolerance is defined	Lower error rate to 0.5% for correction before shipment	Reduce percentage customer-supplier error by at least 85% for the first year of improvement implementation through customers' support and follow-up of their suppliers' compliance.

Feedback and continuous to the process capability improvement program

Figure 6.2 Assessing process capability to determine and mitigate any gap to continually achieve customer satisfaction.

Acknowledgment to those who performed the data mining for this project: Green Belt Team: Rodolfo Nava, quality engineering manager; Ramiro Chacon, process improvement engineer; Victor Garcia, quality engineer; Jorge Molina, quality assurance specialist; Mariann Kay, document control; and Riley McGaughey, operations regional coach Champion: Chris Blunk, chief operations officer, ProTrans

(Chart and example used with permission from the team.)

A Tool for Achieving Operational Compliance and Excellence

The chart in Figure 6.2 shows a case study of a multifunctional team's (operations and quality departments) collaborative efforts to support operational compliance and excellence to satisfy the stakeholders. In this example, the team measured the error rate potentially contributed by the customer-supplier's noncompliance versus the quantified voice of the customer. The focus of the example is to share a simple model in assessing process capability to determine and mitigate any gap to continually achieve customer satisfaction.

Lessons Learned

QMS operational compliance and excellence within the processes' main foundations include management support, workforce buy-in, and strong and time-tested QMS initiatives to sustain continuous customer satisfaction and business growth. Without these elements intertwined together, the QMS will deteriorate and ultimately collapse.

Auditor's Perspective

A sustainable QMS includes self-monitoring of operational compliance to ensure continuing effectiveness regardless of an audit. The compliance is coming from within the organization and is not dictated by customer or market pressure. This feature is an ideal perspective to give any auditor or customer to provide a high confidence level on the QMS integrity without the "policing force" of the audit program. How can a company achieve this positive perspective? Here are a few ways:

- Provide evidence on items being evaluated and include the continuous improvement underway for that particular area or process. It is an old-school mentality to only answer what is being asked by an auditor during audits. Yes, this still happens, but the added mention of ongoing continuous improvements can be beneficial, especially if the area or process under audit is not at 100 percent capability.

- Maintain the visibility of the area/process/system risks identified via PGW or hidden factory assessments through a dynamic documentation (such as the PGW log) including but not limited to the impact, risk mitigation plans, measures of actions' effectiveness, etc. This will not only be beneficial in tackling internal continuous improvement but will also serve as evidence of due diligence in sustaining a dynamic QMS. Be open and honest with the auditor when certain areas are noted as needing improvement; always be prepared to share the containment or improvement plan associated with areas in this category. A dynamic QMS and proper performance indicators should have proactively identified these elements and not have waited for discovery by the auditor. If no plans exist, then it is time to address creating a plan.

- These are just examples of cultivating operational compliance and excellence within the system—there are many more. The critical part is the acknowledgment when failures or improvement opportunities are discovered. Do not cover them, recognize the revelation, and work on the resolution.

7

Resolution of Nonconformances to Maintain Integrity of the QMS and Preserve a Positive Auditor's Review

■──■

The identification, containment, and correction of nonconformities come from different scenarios, and resolutions vary depending on the quality requirements governing any given company as well as that company's direction. The examples in this chapter are based on the integration of both internal and external auditors' input.

The series of examples that follow are depicted in a cartoon-like format to give the readers an approach to the material beyond pure text. The identity of the companies, customers, and parties involved have been changed, converted into *The Adventures of Inspector Leanne N. Green* to preserve the confidentiality of all involved.

The character of Inspector Leanne N. Green was first introduced by author Janet Smith as a running quality lessons learned series in the newsletter of a previous employer. This style sometimes brings an interesting and more approachable angle to the presentation of some of the quality topics.

Note to the readers: Figures 7.1–7.3 on the following pages focus on showing issues, possible root causes, and potential actions. There are other feasible actions and methodologies available for addressing the issues in the examples that are not covered in this chapter. The case studies are merely for demonstration; they are just examples to depict the use of a particular quality tool.

Issue:

Inspector Leanne N. Greene was sent to the assembly line for light fixtures that were returned due to a wrong, non-critical assembly part. The control in place was the color coding of a matching part and assembly. The lane where the errors were taking place had a good success history except for the last two holiday seasons, during which the product was returned repeatedly in a seemingly random frequency.

Inspector Greene started the investigation by reviewing the quality records of the returns.

Inspector Greene used the 6Ms analysis to review any changes or trends of the core internal process variables impacting output, as shown below:

Note: 6Ms analysis is a quality tool listing the input variables common in any process. The "**M**" stands for **M**anpower, **M**ethod, **M**achine, **M**aterial, **M**easurement and **M**other Nature. Knowing the impact of these variables will help in the root cause analysis.

The results pointed to a trend: the same temporary assembler was associated with the returns. It was determined that the temporary assembler was colorblind, affecting the requirement in a random frequency.

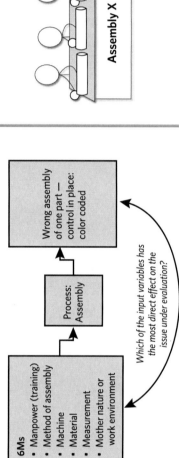

6Ms
- Manpower (training)
- Method of assembly
- Machine
- Material
- Measurement
- Mother nature or work environment

Process: Assembly

Wrong assembly of one part — control in place: color coded

Which of the input variables has the most direct effect on the issue under evaluation?

Assembly X

Figure 7.1 The adventures of Inspector Leanne N. Green: Process requirements and training effectiveness.

Lessons Learned

- CTQ process requirements must be clearly defined. Example tools include documented information such as checklists, etc.
- One quality tool that can be used in identifying root causes is the 6Ms analysis shown in this case study. Think backwards: start with the problem and examine through the process of elimination to determine which process input has a direct association with the issue. In some cases, there may be more than one root cause.
- Training is not completed until training effectiveness verification has been completed. In this case, the process control (i.e., color coding) did not work because training verification may not have been properly performed for temporary holiday workers.

In this case, an eye examination was added to the qualification requirements; other processes dependent on the physical features of the workforce (e.g., weightlifting, etc.) were re-evaluated to prevent a similar situation.

Issue:
Inspector Leanne N. Greene was called to audit the company's new and bigger warehouse for an existing process that was transferred from another building. This initiative was meant to facilitate growth for next year; however, within a month, the new warehouse was incurring 30 percent more overtime and a higher rate of error compared with the process performance in the old building. Inspector Leanne N. Green was sent to the new warehouse to find the root cause of this observation.

Inspector Greene started the investigation by reviewing the volume records and floor activities with the warehouse manager.

The results pointed to a trend: the same temporary assembler was associated with the returns. It was determined that the temporary assembler was colorblind, affecting the requirement in a random frequency.

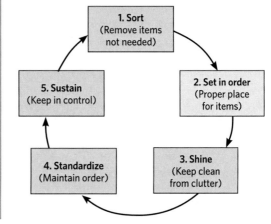

Figure 7.2 The adventures of Inspector Leanne N. Green: 5S program (5S—Sort, Set in Order, Shine, Standardize, and Sustain—is a quality tool for increasing the effectiveness and efficiency of a system).

Lessons Learned

- Start simple. Internal wastes within the control of the company are an easy starting point in the analysis of inefficiencies and improvement opportunities. Available quality tools, such as the 5S used in this case study, can be deployed to monitor and measure excessive wastes before venturing to a more extensive initiative.

- Benchmarking to assess the effectiveness of the 5S system may include cycle time before and after the implementation of the 5S program, and productivity or ULE exerted for certain tasks, e.g., comparison of output between shifts, etc.

Issue:
Inspector Leanne N. Greene was asked to do a gap analysis to investigate a new product line due to performance deterioration after five months of launching. On-time delivery was trending negatively, causing customer concern.

Inspector Greene started the gap analysis by reviewing the process requirements with the account manager responsible for the project using the contract as the reference document.

The contract requirements were verified through review of records and observation of the core process associated with the issue. It was detected that there was *scope creep*; that is, requirements were added after everyone signed off on the contract. The scope creep may have occurred inadvertently or may have been due to the lack of process control in place to prevent the situation.

Customer requirements were not clearly verified during the contract review; during launch, it was discovered there were process difficulties that were not considered or not visible until the actual operations hand-off.

Figure 7.3 The adventures of Inspector Leanne N. Green: Scope creep (no process control for prevention).

Lessons Learned

Following are a couple of key guidelines for new launches, regardless of industry:

- Use a process flowchart. In some cases, process specifications alone may not reveal the potential roadblocks. A process flowchart is a simple tool for identifying core processes during contract review.

- Use layered metrics. The process flowchart can help uncover the processes needing layered metrics. The use of layered metrics allows for measuring the performance of the core processes and the supporting subprocesses. For example, the overtime metric may be an indication of roadblocks being encountered by the workforce to meet certain requirements (such as on-time delivery). In a worst-case scenario, on-time delivery can only be achieved at the cost of overtime due to wastes in the process.

Auditor's Perspective

The discussions in this chapter focus on the resolution of deviations or nonconformances with a negative impact on the integrity of the QMS. The QMS design may have features to proactively identify and resolve nonconformances, but it is not a guarantee that the QMS has identified the possible failure modes in its industry. An auditor's interpretation of a quality standard may be the element that reveals undetected "cracks in the armor." For example, a nonconformance may have been corrected in one situation, but the process owners failed to verify the risk or possibility of a repeating occurrence on a similar product line or process. Although no other recurrence is evident on a similar product or system, failure to include this risk assessment will likely be noted by the auditor. Incorporation of this proactive risk assessment will not only satisfy the auditor's needs but will also enhance the system's nonconformance prevention.

An auditor's perspective not only focuses on the resolution of actual nonconformances impacting the system, but it also looks at the prevention of an impending failure that could be avoided through the installation of proper detection mechanisms. While such an observation may not necessarily be an audit nonconformance, it very possibly could be an improvement opportunity.

This book does not aim to categorize the auditor's audit observation. Therefore, the use of the words "audit finding," "audit nonconformance," or "audit improvement opportunity" are used to describe the auditor's perspective; these words are not meant to be used as official connotation of the auditor's report terminology.

8

Process Performance—Indicators of QMS, Customer, and Auditor Satisfaction

Is the statement "If it's not broken, don't fix it" a good business rule?

The answer is dependent on the performance metrics. If the process is at its optimum capacity in satisfying all the stakeholders' interests and running smoothly, then, yes, this statement may be a logical business rule. However, in cases where the process is consistently running at a very inefficient and below-expectations level, then it is "broken."

"Broken" processes can only be detected if there is visibility to the system; otherwise, we're talking about a hidden factory, a process slowly deteriorating that will eventually cause failure without notice.

How do you prevent a failure from a hidden factory that typically occurs without advance notice? The hidden factory must first be identified.

"ID ME" (Identify Me)

Failure of processes without notice can be prevented using three simple steps, coined as ID ME:

- **ID**entification of core processes
  Which processes are critical? For example, for a medical-device manufacturing clean room, the core processes may be proper gowning, compliance with regulations (such as no debris from contributing articles such as plants brought into the clean room), etc.

- **M**easurement of performance
  Level of performance is not visible without measurements. The performance measurement of the above example (i.e., integrity of the clean room) may be the particle count in parts per million (in comparison with the clean-room certification level).

- Escalation program
  Measurement is not enough if it does not trigger action. For the measurement case above, there should be an action level defined before the particle level reaches nonconformance against the certification's allowable maximum level. Reaching an action level may trigger, for example, an audit of the clean room to verify debris or other contributing factor causing the trending.

What comes after identification and measurement of process performance level?

Identification and measurement of process performance are wasted efforts if data remain static and are not transformed into improvement opportunities.

Improvement opportunities or projects are sometimes challenging to initiate if the process performance level is not easily visible to the workforce. The workforce's management has the primary responsibility of ensuring the initiatives that are selected align with the company's vision. But alignment of these initiatives with the company's vision comes from different sources within the operation. Following are two case studies to demonstrate that the identification of process performance improvement opportunities through the recognition of the symptoms (such as trends) and understanding the voice of the system through metrics analysis.

Example 8.1: Invoicing delay

Scenario: Unpaid invoices representing a significant dollar amount and impacting the company cash flow prompted an audit of the invoicing process to determine the root cause and find a resolution of the problem. It was common knowledge within the accounting department that most of the invoicing delays were due to missing paperwork; however, there was no visibility on the breakdown of the failure. Below is the result of the audit:

- **Process being measured:** Accounting—unpaid invoices.

- **Invoicing metric/goal:** The age of unpaid invoices should not be more than 15 days after service completion.

- **Current status:** More than 85 percent of pending invoices are over 15 days due to missing paperwork.

- **Findings:** The metric for invoicing (i.e., age of unpaid invoice) only shows the invoicing backlog but does not provide enough information on the performance of the associated subprocesses directly impacting the paperwork.

A simple flowchart in Figure 8.1 shows the subprocess breakdown of the hidden factory. Reminder: Hidden factories are variables that have a negative impact on the success of a process that are not easily visible to management or the system.

The operational steps prior to invoicing prioritized completion of the orders to meet the productivity metric. Paperwork verification was not part of the metric at this stage; thus, it was not prioritized, resulting in a delay at the invoicing stage.

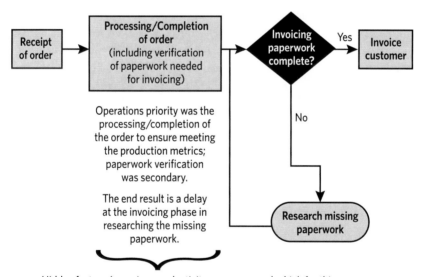

Hidden factory (meaning, productivity measure may be high for this process, but the incomplete paperwork is hidden and became visible at another phase).

What secondary metrics could have prevented the hidden factory of Figure 8.1?

A metric on the complete paperwork hand-off to the next process will help the early detection of any missing paperwork prior to the invoicing process. This will increase the accountability of the process owners in securing the needed paperwork, as well as the timely and accurate submission of invoices to customers.

Figure 8.1 Sample DMAIC path to help achieve operational compliance and excellence within a process.

Example 8.2: Process does not appear "broken" but a closer look detected inefficiency

Scenario: The facility manager of one of five plants consistently reported performance within the metric required by management, with the exception of excessive overtime. Other than the overtime, the facility manager believed his process was not "broken." The overtime incurred was explained as due to customer increased volume; the facility manager was awaiting additional resources. Before approval of additional resources, management requested an independent QA gap analysis to verify if there was something "broken" in the process.

Table 8.1 shows the results of the gap analysis reflecting that overtime could have been avoided if proper allocation of resource was aligned with the customer demand, a metric that could have shown the resource demand forecast. In summary, the system was broken. The gap analysis using root cause analysis detected the improvement opportunity needed.

Problem / Bottleneck	Impact	Evidence / Sample	Root Cause	Recommended Action
Customer requirement was not properly aligned with the plant's capability and resource allocation, causing poor planning.	Overtime is incurred to prevent delay or missed delivery schedule.	Trailers with varying volume arrive throughout the day without required cut-off time for processing. This is a setup for failure in meeting customer processing time.	Customer requirement not clearly reviewed to ensure center will be successful in meeting customer specifications, for example: • Cycle time not defined. • No cut-off time set with customer.	Customer requirement versus cycle time was evaluated to restructure cut-off time to be compatible with plant resource schedule and customer requirement. A secondary metric should be considered (e.g., cycle time or cut-off compliance).

Table 8.1 A gap analysis using root cause analysis can detect a needed improvement opportunity.

Lessons Learned

In plain view, productivity or any other performance metric may not always show the big picture. Primary metrics need continuous validation to ensure a balanced scorecard approach. Selection and deployment of the key process indicators (KPIs) should consider the voice of the process and the voice of the customer to truly understand the risks and benefits involved in this activity (Smith 2012b).

- A simple breakdown of the subprocesses, as shown in Table 8.1, will help visualize the origin of the roadblocks. In both examples, the substandard execution of the prior processes gave a false impression of impressive productivity metrics, hiding the roadblocks.

- A secondary metric, as applicable, is beneficial in creating balance in the system and helps in the prevention of hidden factories.

A system may seem "unbroken," but if there are other indicators showing potential issues, verify its integrity. It can be a simple gap analysis following the performance indicators.

Auditor's Perspective

A QMS may have identified indicators of a successful performance but may still be cited by the auditor as non-satisfactory or needing improvement. A QMS, in most cases, may not be able to recognize all the criteria needed to satisfy an auditor's perspective due to the many variables in the process. How does one win this seemingly losing scenario?

It is true that a QMS may not be able to achieve a one-size-fits-all model—there's always the chance that an outlier may suddenly make an unexpected entrance during an audit. This is not an unusual event. An example is a stable process with stable parameters that suddenly shows continuous rejects while under audit. What do you do? You may be sweating at that moment trying hard to remain on the good side of the auditor. That should not be the case. Keep in mind that you or the process owners are the subject experts on this matter; therefore, you or the process owners should know the process like the back of your hand. Therefore, the ideal action is to execute what you or the process owners normally do in events like this one. Changing the tasks for the auditor's sake is the riskiest response, as that may pose safety risks, error risks, etc. The audit arena is not an acting platform—be yourself. The lesson learned is: Do what you say you are doing, and, if there is a need for change, follow the typical steps of change management.

9

Auditing Beyond Compliance—
A Dynamic Tool to Foster Synergy Among
the QMS, Customer, and Auditor's Perspectives

Strategic planning, process metrics, risk mitigation, and auditing are key elements of any business, and all intertwine to support business goals. These fundamental business quality components are variables that should be considered in the implementation of an audit program (see Figure 9.1). They serve as additional cross-checks in verifying its effectiveness. Auditing that is focused only on the "compliance verification box" will miss identifying improvement opportunities outside this box. The solution is to go beyond the box using the auditing beyond compliance model.

Strategic planning

Process metrics

Risk mitigation

Auditing

Figure 9.1 The strategic planning, process metrics, risk mitigation, and auditing interrelationship form the foundation of a successful business model.

(ASQ Audit Division 2016)

Auditing Beyond Compliance

When undertaking auditing beyond compliance, the first thing to keep in mind is: Go beyond the visible symptoms you can see; there may be hidden factories causing the symptoms. Some quality professionals limit their focus to the verification of compliance, as it is not always apparent how to implement the other strength of the auditing function (i.e., a tool for identifying improvement opportunities). This approach of limiting auditing to compliance verification may originate in the attitude: "I have no authority to change the process, my job is to audit the process to ensure compliance." Such a philosophy and its restricted mindset will cause missed opportunities in the auditing process, but this attitude may have originated in a lack of tools to express the value of auditing beyond compliance, as shown in Table 9.1.

Comparison	
Auditing Beyond Compliance	**Compliance Verification Audit**
Finding: The oven in Line 1 is used once a year due to a recent volume decrease over the last two years. During the audit, the oven was out of calibration. **Action:** The process manager needs to assess if there is an efficient option to process the low-volume demand for Line 1 (e.g., shared use of other available ovens).	**Finding:** The oven dedicated for Line 1 require calibration every six months. During the audit, it was found to be past the calibration date, a violation of the process requirement. **Action:** The process manager will coordinate calibration of the oven.

Table 9.1 Comparison between the auditing beyond compliance (ABC) model versus the more typical compliance verification audit model.

The two scenarios in Table 9.1 show the advantage of using the auditing beyond compliance (ABC) model over the more typical compliance verification audit model. In the first example, there is a situation that needs mitigation in order to optimize the available ovens rather than continuing to dedicate an oven to a low-volume demand, which is a waste of resources, a hidden factory. Another depiction of the ABC model in Figure 9.2 shows how it can also strengthen the QMS structure and contribute to a positive auditor's perspective. While perception may play as a friend or foe depending on the situation, one thing is sure—a strong perception may last a long time (i.e., the entire duration of an audit) and may impact the outcome of the audit.

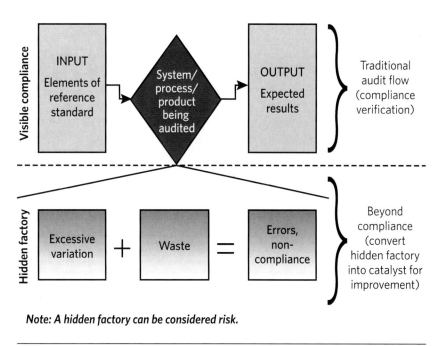

Note: A hidden factory can be considered risk.

Figure 9.2 Model of auditing beyond compliance.

(Smith 2012a)

There are many more examples of hidden factories or risks fitting this model—too many to mention in this book. The guiding force is the recognition of waste and the opportunity for improvement benefiting all stakeholders. Remember: In general, a business cannot spend a million dollars to gain a few hundred. Logic and risk assessment have to guide decision-making toward what is most effective and efficient.

It is a waste of an improvement opportunity to not consider the implementation of the auditing beyond compliance approach, regardless of company size, product, service, or customer base. This can be a concept that is more difficult to digest for hardcore compliance audit supporters, but we urge all to try it.

Figure 9.3 shows the different levels of the auditing beyond compliance implementation.

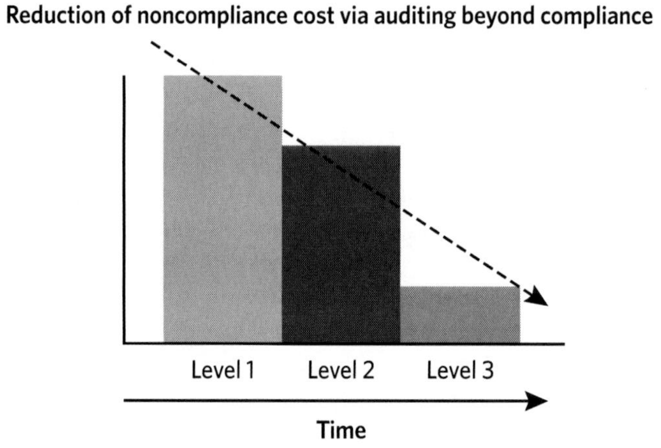

Reduction of noncompliance cost via auditing beyond compliance

Level 1—Process owners' compliance buy-in is not consistent, a fluctuating quality level. This is the most expensive phase if basic compliance is not in effect.

Level 2—Process owners' buy-in is consistent with compliance, self-regulating. Start reduction of costs associated with nonconformances. This phase will give more opportunities to provide improvement initiatives.

Level 3—Beyond compliance: improvement, sustainability, and cost savings. Once compliance is achieved, improvement initiatives are easier to deploy and measure.

Figure 9.3 Phases of implementing auditing beyond compliance.

Figures 9.4–9.8 show an easy step-by-step tutorial[7] to aid your implementation of auditing beyond compliance. Note that there are common steps with the traditional compliance audit.

---

[7] The tutorial and example are from the ASQ webinar "Auditing Beyond Compliance" (October 7, 2015).

ABC planning highlights
E.g., process to be audited: Pizza baking process

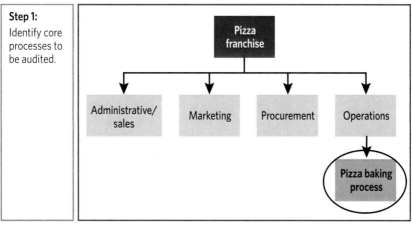

Step 1:
Identify core processes to be audited.

Figure 9.4 Step 1: Identify core processes to be audited.

ABC planning highlights

Step 2:
Create simple input/output flowchart of the core process to be audited.

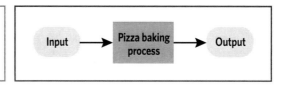

Figure 9.5 Step 2: Create simple input/output flowchart of the core process to be audited.

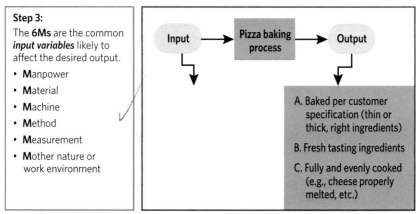

Figure 9.6 Step 3: Evaluate the 6Ms as the common input variables likely to affect the desired output.

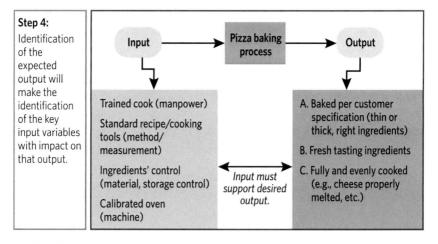

Figure 9.7 Step 4: Check the impact of input variables on desired output.

ABC planning highlights

Without metrics, it is difficult to measure progress; traditional compliance audit scope does not necessarily cover the measure of success.

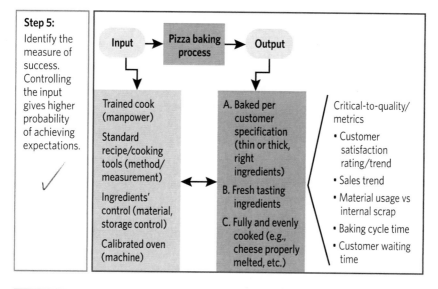

Figure 9.8 Step 5: Identify the measures of success. Without metrics, it is difficult to measure progress.

The goal of the tutorial's pizza exercise was to show the simple steps in the implementation of the ABC model. This process can be part of the pre-audit planning and data mining through process owner survey/interview, review of the work instructions, etc. The data collection can be part of the "audit checklist." Data collected can be summarized and formatted using a template, as in Table 9.2. This document may then become part of the audit report to track findings/improvement opportunities.

Sample format input/output and metrics for the pizza process sample				
A. Element	**B. Critical-to-quality**	**C. Success factor**	**D. Measure of success**	**E. Possible evidence**
Manpower	Cook	Training/ competency	Success rate	Log record
Material	Ingredients	Freshness	Acceptance rate	Inspection log
Machine	Oven	Temperature setting	Temperature gauge	Calibration records
Method	Preparation	Repeatable recipe	Waste rate	Material inventory
Measurement	Scale	Repeatable/ accurate	etc.	etc.
Environment	Ingredients' storage	Reliability	etc.	etc.

Table 9.2 Sample template for summarizing and formatting data collected in the simple steps of the demonstrated auditing beyond compliance tool.

Another option for summarizing the auditing beyond compliance results is an ABC template. Figure 9.9 shows the quality element being audited. Any standard can be used as a reference point with this tool.

The use of the template demonstrated in Figure 9.9 offers these benefits:

- It eliminates the need for lengthy verbiage during the report writing, minimizing the burden on those who are not natural writers; the template focuses on critical observations rather than long narrative explanations.

- It increases the visibility of seeing the critical elements and CTQ pieces of each process without the clutter of words.

- It provides easy and visible tracking of open items.

- The template may be used as the actual audit report; if there is a mandated audit form to be used, this template can be attached to the report as added work notes.

Auditing Beyond Compliance Template
Applicable to any standard

Box A	Box B	Box C	Box D	Box E	Box F	Box G	Box H
Core element (breakdown of core elements into sub-elements)	**Sub-element** (breakdown of core elements)	**Critical-to-Quality (CTQ)** (examples of factors to meet intent of element being audited)	**Evidence** (proof of existence and/or deployment — show me)	**Measure effectiveness** XXXXXXXX	**Measure of success** XXXXXXXX	**Identified waste** XXXXXXXX	**Identify or verify savings** XXXXXXXX
	Process/elements being audited	Compliance verification		Improvement implementation			
Pizza baking procedural requirements: • Manpower training—xxx • Machine calibration requirement—xxx • Process cycle—xxx Observed 1st & 2nd shifts, Team 1-2 No observations	ISO elements xxx requirements verified: (Documentation, Quality Records, Calibration) against observation of Team 1, 1st & 2nd shift, Oven xx. No observations	Critical-to-Quality (CTQ) noted on procedure xxx, such as ZZZ, observed during 1st shift, Oven zz: **Observation:** CTQ xx, not matching quality records resuts period xx.	Evidence verified: Batch Quality records Weight historical records Oven settings vs specifications Calibration records vs specifications **Observation:** Calibration of scale X out of spec. causing miscalculation of raw materials and shortage by 25%.	XXXXXXXX	XXXXXXXX	XXXXXXXX	XXXXXXXX

Reference standard: Pizza baking process work instructions xx & ISO 9001:2015

Figure 9.9 Sample ABC report template using ISO 9001:2015 as its reference point.

(Auditing Beyond Compliance, 2012)

Lessons Learned

An auditing beyond compliance approach brings added value to the auditing function benefitting the entire enterprise. Compliance is a critical part of protecting the interest of the stakeholders; extending this role beyond compliance is an even greater value in that it contributes to financial growth, process improvement, workforce development, and continuing customer satisfaction.

Using the simple tools featured in this chapter—the five-step process to implement the auditing beyond compliance model and the auditing beyond compliance report template—will help those involved transition from the traditional compliance audit to auditing beyond compliance.

Auditor's Perspective

The auditing beyond compliance model discussed in this chapter aims to cover the wide spectrum of auditing and beyond. However, some QMS elements may still be left exposed, "unprotected," from the auditor's perspective, depending on the situation.

Although internal audit findings may be properly addressed with action plans, multiple reoccurrences of the same incidents will likely raise an alert. An auditor may conclude that action plans were ineffective, or problems were not properly identified. To avoid this negative auditor's take, the QMS should include a review of the following key elements:

- A check that problems listed versus actions assigned are relevant
- A periodic review of trends
- Actions to take if trends are detected, with notes about reasons no action was taken (for example, management's business decision or customer approval)
- Verification of actions' effectiveness

The list above is just a fragment of an auditor's potential perspective on this element. Maintain an open mind, with the attitude that the auditor's perspective is an additional resource for improvement ideas.

10

Management Review—Critical Support for QMS Success and Auditor's Acceptance

Management review seems to be one of the QMS elements that is difficult to decipher, as it is subject to many interpretations. Published journals and business partners have provided ample commentary regarding the challenges of implementing a lean, effective, and sustainable management review. One possible reason for the difficulty of implementing a successful management review is the lack of understanding about its true role in the business.

This muddled grasp of management review prompted the dedication of this chapter to a simple and effective model, one that has been critiqued, complimented, and "tumble polished" by both internal and external auditors under different standards. It is ready for use.

Management review is simpler than it sounds, and this chapter will present the model in a simplistic way. Our treatment will show a logical breakdown of the model so it can be easily understood and converted to deliverables. We will concentrate on the understanding and management of a generic management review's compliance and documentation strategies. Once these strategies are learned, the knowledge may be applied to any type of management review input/output. The aim of this chapter is not to determine specific input/output under a specific standard (such as ISO)—our goal is *not to give a fish to the process owner* but rather to *teach the process owner how to fish.*[8]

Let's begin.

What is management review?

Every process or system, including the management review, has input and output variables. Simply put, the management review is a process that acts

---

[8] Extracted from Management Review 2018 meeting presentation by Gary Cardenas, President, ProTrans/3PL company.

as an overseer of the inputs and outputs of the system that ensures all variables are properly balanced to meet stakeholders' expectations (see Figure 10.1).

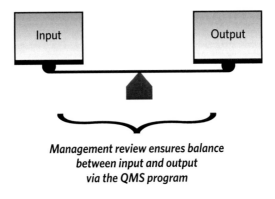

Management review ensures balance between input and output via the QMS program

Figure 10.1 Bare minimum representation of a management review.

Why is management review needed in a business?

As mentioned previously, management review is an overview function that ensures success of the input and output variables. Otherwise, the processes or system becomes like a sailboat without a sail, randomly blown by the wind in various directions. When this happens, results are not beneficial, and an organization can expect such things as misaligned goals, financial loss, customer dissatisfaction, etc. This chaos is prevented by management review through different tools under the QMS umbrella balancing the input/output variables.

What are the input and output variables of a management review process, and how are they determined?

In some quality standards (such as the ISO standard), there are specific mandated input and output aspects of management review.

In other cases, these inputs/outputs need to be determined. Thinking backwards is one technique for defining them. Define the expected output first, then go back and list the variables that will provide success for each item in the output column to identify the input needed.

Table 10.1 provides examples of other sources of the inputs/outputs for businesses complying with multiple quality standards or internal and/or customer requirements.

Input →	Management Review →	Output
Examples of influencing factors that will dictate the input and output of the management review process	• Business direction/ management vision • Market demand • Regulatory governance • Technology/ process availability • Financial capability	Management review process continually evaluates the input and output variables to detect and mitigate the gap between the two sets of variables.	• Stakeholders' satisfaction • Target market share • Compliance to regulatory requirements • Competitive technology acquisition • Financial wealth/stability

Table 10.1 Other influencing factors to determine input/output.

How does a company show evidence of compliance with the management review elements (i.e., input/output variables)?

Once a company has determined the input/output variables required or desired for its business, the next step is to document those variables to standardize the documentation of evidence that is needed to show compliance, either with a regulatory governance or a customer requirement. It can be a controlled document log listing the inputs/outputs and evidence (see Table 10.2).

The selection of evidence of compliance has a wide array of variation. To demonstrate that the documented information associated with the element is to-date, we suggest attaching it as part of the evidence. While documented information is not always mandatory, we recommend including it, as it is a good default for the standardization of information relay.

The following examples show a wide array of evidence of compliance[9] that may be included to show due diligence and compliance with the input/output elements:

- For a traceability element, evidence may include quality records showing compliance with traceability such as batch records, serial number records, shipment/delivery records, raw material lot number traceable to batch records, recorded complaint of a returned product with evidence of analysis and disposition (e.g., scrapped), etc.

[9] Some of the elements mentioned in the following list are input/output elements from the ISO standard's management review.

Input elements	Evidence of compliance (list attachment reference number, or hyperlink)	Brief description of evidence	Additional comments or status (e.g., completion status, timeline, etc.)
Element 1-XX			
Element 2-XX			
Element 3-XX			
Element 4-XX			
Etc.			
Output elements			
Element 1-XX			
Element 2-XX			
Element 3-XX			
Element 4-XX			
Etc.			

Table 10.2 Example of an input/output evidence log for management review.

- For a customer feedback element, evidence may include an actual customer feedback analysis and closure, log of the feedback received for the last six months, trend analysis showing actions taken to address a starting trend, etc.

- For a continuous improvement element, evidence may include a log of ongoing improvement plans or projects, an actual project completion, etc.

- For a segregation of nonconforming material element, evidence may include line clearance record, batch records accounting for rejected parts transferred to the rejection log, etc.

- For an effectiveness of action element, evidence may include documented results of a change resulting from a corrective action (e.g., cycle-time reduction, thereby avoiding shipment delay), etc.

- For a change management element, evidence may include a validation report log before approval of a change, log of changed documents with evidence of review and approval, training records for a new process, etc.

- For a management involvement or participation in the management review element, evidence may include meeting minutes and agendas showing discussions of quality elements, such as review of a customer contract, email/communication from leadership regarding business direction or performance or metrics, announcement of company changes, etc.

- For an internal communication element, evidence may include internal news media to announce company changes and internal news, periodic departmental meetings regarding various business topics such as human resources, new processes, new customer launch, etc.

- For a customer focus element, evidence may include workshops held for and attended by customers, an improvement plan specific to the customer as part of contract renewal, site-visit minutes for improvement discussions, trend analysis reports of an account specific to a customer inquiry on performance, etc.

- For a performance of external providers element, evidence may include business partners' scorecard (if any), communication (e.g., email) regarding review of performance relating to contract renewal, training on a company's new communication portal requirements, etc.

- For an internal audit element, evidence may include documented PGWs discussed in previous chapters of this book. (Ensure open observations have follow-up or closure timeline.)

- For a resource needs element, evidence may include productivity monitoring and evaluation of manpower for certain processes, etc.

- For a status of previous management review's open-items element, evidence may include documented follow-up and timeline of closure (if still open, list root causes or actions under evaluation), etc.

- For a customer satisfaction element, evidence may include positive survey results (if any), commendation or letter of appreciation from customer, site-visit minutes, etc.

The key to the selection of evidence is the understanding of the input/output variables. It is not a difficult task to retrieve and gather the information; with today's electronic communication technologies, details of evidence are everywhere. One just needs to know what to collect (e.g., pictures or electronic copies of documents).

How often is the evidence collected and documented on a template like the one in Table 10.2?

The management review process, contrary to the once-a-year practice during earlier years of quality standards requirements, may be performed on an incremental, ongoing basis, covering all the required elements within the required period (for example, annually). What does this mean? This means completion of verifying evidence within the time frame in question, as shown in Figure 10.2. This is the same concept as the incremental self-audit, i.e., the PGW discussed in Chapter 4.

Figure 10.2 shows an example of a quarterly incremental review of the input/output elements spread over the course of a year. The incremental review frequency is at the discretion of the designated gatekeeper.

At the end of each review period (e.g., quarterly), a brief summary report should be issued to the designated management review team as status notification to indicate continuing effectiveness or incompletion due to roadblocks (e.g., a long period needed to close open complaints). The template used in Table 10.2 may be issued to management as evidence of management notification.

Concerns or findings noted should be mitigated and addressed; as needed, an internal corrective action request may be issued to document and track the progress of open item closure.

Who is responsible for the coordination and documentation of the management review process?

Typically, the gatekeeper is from the QA department, as management review resembles the audit function; however, it can be assigned to a qualified independent role at the discretion of the company.

1st quarter Input elements xx Output elements xx	2nd quarter Input elements xx Output elements xx
3rd quarter Input elements xx Output elements xx	4th quarter Input elements xx Output elements xx

Figure 10.2 Example of one way to document incremental management review.

Has this method been proven acceptable to external/ regulatory audits?

The management review method referenced in this chapter consists of these components:

- Determination of the input/output variables depending on the quality standard governing the business

- Summarizing the evidence of compliance for each required input/output

- Incremental review of the above using the PGW approach

The author has been given permission by ProTrans 3PL company to disclose ProTrans's use of the PGW and the incremental documentation of the management review throughout the year (i.e., Template 10.1—Management Review), both of which have been audited and accepted by its ISO registrar and C-TPAT auditors. The management review methods and the processes/documentation resulting from the use of the methods have been audited multiple times, resulting in ProTrans's consistent ISO and C-TPAT recertifications.

With that said, remember to maintain an awareness of the varying company-specific or quality standards governing your organization to ensure compatibility of the models' coverage with those requirements. There is a blank template in the Template section that follows this chapter to assist with this activity.

Lessons Learned

Management review is one of the critical elements of a QMS. A QMS may be elegantly designed, but without the verifiable support of management, there is no power in the QMS engine. The management review program also relies on the design of initiatives and alignment of verifiable evidence of compliance based on the company's interpretations of the regulatory requirements (e.g., ISO).

There is a simple model for the verification of management review described in this chapter.[10] This may be used as a reference in the creation of a management review model that may be modified to customize per the company's requirements. Do not reinvent the wheel.

Auditor's Perspective

A QMS designer may think a perfect management review has been established in the designed QMS until a loophole is discovered during an audit. This should not create a concern—it is an opportunity for improvement. Some examples of loopholes to avoid and address to maintain a positive stakeholder and auditor perspective include the following:

- The QMS designer should ensure a system for periodic verification that all management review elements consistently take place. (This is also called management buy-in.) Without this buy-in secured at the beginning of the QMS design, the QMS will likely fail. Keep the program simple and easy to implement with key personnel as gatekeepers to ensure continuing effectiveness.

- Significant repeating trends in performance metrics may have been recorded, but if not acted upon, may be deemed as a finding during an audit. If the trend is not significant to the performance metrics, the company should reconsider if the metric should be revised or if a more meaningful data collection that triggers action should be chosen.

- When using the PGW method (i.e., incremental) to evaluate trends, ensure review data cover the entire management review cycle. For example, if a PGW of the management review process is done on a quarterly basis, ensure the 12-month data review is completed for an annual management review cycle.

---

[10] "Commendation for Best Practice" was issued by C-TPAT on ProTrans's 2017 validation audit report for use of the PGW. The C-TPAT office/auditor also gave permission to that statement, as we did earlier in the book.

Templates

List of templates to follow:

Template 1.1   Identification of Core Processes for Business Unit or Process

Template 2.1   Creation of Layered Metrics—Core and Subprocesses

Template 6.1   Continuous Improvement Projects Log—For Operational Excellence

Template 7.1   Identification, Containment, and Resolution of Nonconformances

Template 9.1   Kaizens Resulting from Auditing Beyond Compliance

Template 10.1 Management Review—Documentation of Input and Output Evidence

Template 1.1 Identification of Core Processes for Business Unit or Process

This template may be used to identify the core steps or processes being performed by a business unit or function for the following, but not limited to:

- Review of process for accuracy or documentation update
- Pre-survey tool prior to an audit of an area
- Identification of areas needing metrics or update

Process under evaluation: _____

Department: _____

Prepared by (name and role): _____

Date: _____

List core functions or processes (using simple bullet points is acceptable); adjust the form's rows/columns as needed.

Core processes in this department, with metric	Frequency/ volume	Is there existing documented information for the reference?	Comments/ roadblocks
Example: Receiving process: Receive and verify incoming material from approved suppliers	Avg: 10 shipments per day; 30 minutes to process per shipment	Yes: Flowchart, Document # xxx	Documented information obsolete, needs to be updated Open

Template 2.1   Creation of Layered Metrics—Core and Subprocesses

This template may be used to document the subprocesses that are associated with a core process to evaluate if layered metrics are needed (or for brainstorming purposes). It can be used as a log for floor visibility (or internal electronic display) and/or to be reviewed on a regular basis for any actions needed.

Core process under evaluation: _____

Week xx: _____

Prepared by (name and role): _____

Date: _____

List core functions or processes (using simple bullet points is acceptable); adjust the form's rows/columns as needed.

Core processes and their subprocesses performed by the same department	Metric (goal vs. actual)	Is there existing documented information for reference?	Comments/ roadblocks/ actions
Example: Core process: Final assembly Subprocesses: • Pick parts • Line clearance • Machine assembly • Final automatic optical inspection	Overall goal: 600 units per shift Breakdown of metric requirement for each subprocess: • Pick parts • Line clearance • Machine assembly • Final automatic optical inspection	Yes: Flowchart, Document # xxx	January xx metrics for final automatic optical inspection missing during review on xx— will be followed up before end of first quarter, etc.

Template 6.1 Continuous Improvement Projects Log—
For Operational Excellence

This template is to keep a departmental log of the continuous improvement projects for departmental follow-up. Details of the project may already be logged in a central, company-wide portal; this log may be used by the department leader for easy visibility of resource time allocation within the department.

Prepared by (name and role): _____

Date: _____

Department: _____

List core functions or processes (using simple bullet points is acceptable); adjust the form's rows/columns as needed.

Project	Assigned to	Status	Comments
Example: Project: Streamline customer complaint processing Start date: January 2020 Ref: SharePoint project portal	John Smith	On hold	Smith's travel schedule; will resume in three months on xx/xx/xx.

Template 7.1 Identification, Containment, and Resolution of Nonconformances

This template may be used to document/log the nonconforming materials identified to prevent mix up and trace resolution. It is the responsibility of the designated inspector to obtain input from the designated manager as needed. Once status is completed, the item may be crossed out and initialed by quarantine personnel.

Nonconforming material—ID or Tag #	Location	Inspector/ date/reason	Comments/ status
Example: Batch 123—Tag 001	Quarantine area 1	John Smith xx/xx/xx Reason: No shipping box label	• Reported for labeling by shipping department • Completed—ready for release

Template 9.1 Kaizens Resulting from Auditing Beyond Compliance

This template may be used to log and track added value (kaizens) resulting from auditing beyond compliance (ABC) or a process grid walk (PGW). Periodic recognition (e.g., quarterly) of these accomplishments will provide visibility of credit and appreciation of the workforce.

Auditing beyond compliance (ABC) or process grid walk (PGW)	Kaizens (improvements)	Comments/ savings	Status
Example: PGW #201 (xx/xx/xx)— Receiving process	Kaizen 201 —Movement of receiving dock to improve layout (Initiated by John Smith; xx/xx/xx).	Result: 40% reduction of cycle time	Move completed on xx/xx/xx; cycle reduction validated. Closed

Template 10.1 Management Review—Documentation of Input and Output Evidence

This template is to document the verification of evidence for the management review's input and output elements.

Note: Each document should reflect the date within the cycle being reported. If the incremental evaluation method is used, only the selected elements will be reported for that period; however, verification of all the elements must be completed for the annual period.

Instructions: Each element may be verified more than once within the evaluation period; trend results should reflect the annual performance, meaning the trend may be reviewed incrementally for early detection/mitigation (e.g., first quarter) but should be reviewed again (e.g., end of year) to cover the entire evaluation period.

Use hyperlinks or attach electronic copies to this form for easy organization and access. Evidence associated with the listed input/output elements may be gathered at the predetermined incremental period documented on this form.

The designated management team and pertinent process owners should be copied upon distribution of the form on the approved frequency (e.g., quarterly) with appropriate evidence (e.g., email distribution). Adjust the form's columns as needed for customization.

It is the responsibility of the form user to adhere to the company-specific requirements, including the standard governing its QMS. This form is a tool only. Refer to your organization's internal protocol and/or Chapter 10 of this book for further reference and guidance.

(continued)

Template 10.1   Management Review—Documentation of Input and Output Evidence (continued)

Management Review of Input/Output Evidence

Cycle (e.g., Q1): _____Year: ____

A. Input elements	B. Evidence location or hyperlink	C. Brief description of evidence	D. Status/ completed?
Example: PGWs etc.	• PGW procedures identifying team, frequency, etc., maintained in document control archive xx • Team training records kept in training department • Completed PGW reports parallel to schedule maintained in xx portal • etc.	Evidence included: • Master copy of procedures in document control department • Training records • PGW listed actions —completed as verified for timeline xx. • etc.	Completed

(continued)

Template 10.1 Management Review—Documentation of Input and Output Evidence *(continued)*

A. Output elements	B. Evidence location or hyperlink	C. Brief description of evidence	D. Status/ completed?
Corrective actions	Action plans listed in PGW reports timeline xx verified as completed except item xx	Corrective action records xx for timeline xx on portal xx, timeline xx.	Incomplete item will be reverified on next review cycle xx.

Overall evaluation/comments (include if deemed effective or needing actions). If issued incrementally (e.g., quarterly), identify the elements being reported for the period to match the overall evaluation:

_____

_____

_____

Distributed to (list names/roles): _____

_____

_____

_____

By gatekeeper (name/role):_____

Date:_____

Glossary

Auditing Beyond Compliance (ABC). A form of auditing that goes beyond compliance verification to include the identification of wastes and/or improvement opportunities within the audit scope.

core processes. Critical processes crucial to the success of the entire process flow or system, as determined by the process owners or by management. Selection of core processes may be based on financial impact, customer satisfaction, regulatory requirements, etc.

CTQ (critical-to-quality). The variables or specifications critical to the success of a product or process.

eating the elephant one bite at a time. In this book, this phrase reflects dividing a big task into smaller steps or phases to allow completion of the tasks under limited time or resource. This logic also provides an opportunity to observe the process performance under varying scenarios. This is the basis of the Process Grid Walk of a process.

first pass yield. Used in a manufacturing environment to mean the number of accepted units before a rework.

grassroots level. Refers to the hands-on workers who are considered the subject experts of the tasks they are performing.

hidden factory. Waste or anomaly in the system that is not easily visible to management or the workforce; it may refer to anything from a simple to a complex defect with varying impact on the system.

KPI (key performance indicator). A quantifiable metric used to evaluate an organization's performance objectives.

layered metrics. The assignment of metrics for every critical step within a process so there is accountability of supporting process with low performance. This helps focus where improvement efforts should be extended.

line clearance. Checking a line/assembly line to ensure there are no materials or items from previous runs to ensure the integrity of the process and the prevention of mix-up.

pilot run. Experimental/test run. Items or materials in the pilot run are typically not included in the production release.

Process Grid Walk (PGW). A self-audit method performed in incremental steps rather than in one session. The "grid" refers to the scope under evaluation; for example, if there are five business units in the plant, process owners may choose to divide the audit into five grids and perform audits in incremental frequency (e.g., one grid per month). This method gives more visibility to the roadblocks, pains, or hidden factories that are not easily seen by traditional audits.

QMS. Quality management system.

robust QMS. A dynamic QMS; a QMS that accommodates interaction from its users; the opposite of a rigid system that has no flexibility or tools to handle changes or challenges.

subprocess. Any of the individual supporting processes that comprise a core process.

VOC (voice of the customer). Customer feedback to the system.

References

ASQ Audit Division. 2016. "Risk Analysis: Using Auditing Beyond Compliance Method." Presentation at ASQ 25th Annual Audit Division Conference, Memphis, TN, October 19.

Meyer, Pauline. 2019. "Applie Inc.'s Organizational Culture and Its Characteristics (An Analysis)." Panmore Institute. http://panmore.com/apple-inc-organizational-culture-features-implications.

Park, Kyoung S., Abhinav Kapoor, and Jason Leigh. 2000. "Lessons Learned From Employing Multiple Perspectives in a Collaborative Virtual Environment for Visualizing Scientific Data." In *Proceedings of the Third International Conference on Collaborative Virtual Environments*, 73–82. New York: ACM.

Smith, Janet Bautista. 2012a. *Auditing Beyond Compliance: Using The Portable Universal Quality Lean Concept*. Milwaukee, WI: ASQ Quality Press.

Smith, Janet Bautista. 2012b. "The Big Picture—Do Not Be Misled By Productivity Measures." *Quality Progress* (August).

Smith, Janet Bautista. 2012c. "Auditing Beyond Compliance." Presentation at ASQ 21st Audit Conference, Augusta, GA.

Smith, Janet Bautista. 2014. "Intersection of Quality and Lean—Finding Your Hidden Factories." Workshop at Purdue University sponsored by Purdue TAP Group, Indianapolis, IN, July 30–August 6.

Smith, Janet Bautista. 2010. "Lean Express." Presentation at ASQ Lean and Six Sigma Conference, Phoenix, March 8.

Smith, Janet Bautista. 2010. "Rapid Response." *Quality Progress* (July).

Smith, Janet Bautista. 2019. "Starfish and Turtles." *Quality Progress* 52, no. 3: 64.

Smithson, Nathaniel. 2018. "Google's Organizational Culture & Its Characteristics (An Analysis)." Panmore Institute. http://panmore.com/google-organizational-culture-characteristics-analysis.

Bibliography

ASQ/ANSI/ISO 9001:2015: Quality Management Systems - Requirements. Milwaukee, WI: ASQ, 2015.

ASQ Audit Division. "Strategy, Metrics, and Risk Management." 25th Annual ASQ Audit Division Conference, Memphis, TN, October 21, 2016.

Kubiak, Thomas M., and Donald W. Benbow. *The Certified Six Sigma Black Belt Handbook*. Milwaukee, WI: ASQ Quality Press, 2009.

Markowitz, Eric. "Leadership Lessons from Tim Cook," December 2012. https://www.inc.com/eric-markowitz/tim-cooks-message-for-ceos-admit-when-youre-wrong.html.

Mitchell, Joe. "Benchmarking Knowledge." *Quality Progress* (October 2016).

Moreland, Julie. "Steve Jobs, Apple and the Importance of Company Culture," November 2, 2011, https://www.fastcompany.com/1792485/steve-jobs-apple-and-importance-company-culture.

Nelson, T. Dan. "The Gravity of PDCA." *Quality Progress* (January 2017).

Pruitt, W. Frazier. "Disciplined Approach." *Quality Progress* (May 2019).

Smith, Janet Bautista. "Auditing Beyond Compliance." Presentation ASQ Chapter 903, Indianapolis, IN, October 24, 2014.

Smith, Janet Bautista. *Nielda Is Different*. CreateSpace Independent Publishing Platform, 2016.

Smith, Janet Bautista. "Rapid Response." *Quality Progress* (July 2010).

Smith, Janet Bautista. "The Sow's Ear." *Lean and Six Sigma Review* 15, no. 3 (2016): 15.

Smith, Janet Bautista. "Structured in the Shadows." *Six Sigma Forum Magazine* 15, no. 1 (2015).

Smith, Janet Bautista. Hidden Factory, https://videos.asq.org/keyword/janet-bautista-smith.

Smith, J. 2012. "A case of mistaken capability." iSixSigma.com, April 2012. http://www.isixsigma.com/implementation/case-studies/a-case-of-mistaken-capability/.

Smith, J. A model for implementing a 5S program. iSixSigma.com. https://www.isixsigma.com/tools-templates/5s/a-model-for-implementing-a-5s-program/.

Smith, J. An Email and Popcorn and Tsunami Analogy. iSixSigma.com. https://www.isixsigma.com/community/blogs/an-email-and-popcorn-and-tsunami-analogy/.

Smith, Janet. "Lean Auditing." ASQ 19th and 20th Audit Division Conference Workshop, Reno, NV, 2011.

Smith, Janet. "Strategic Planning and Systems Thinking: Business Sector's Perspective Using Lean Methodology." ASQ Education Division Workshop, Louisville, KY, November 2012.

Index

Note: Numbers followed by *f* and *t* indicate figures and tables.

About the Author

Janet Bautista Smith

Janet Bautista Smith has more than 38 years of quality management experience in various manufacturing environments, including the medical device, automotive, and military and logistics industries. Bautista Smith's experience includes hands-on design of quality systems from ground zero through maintenance of the programs. Bautista Smith has incorporated lean and Six Sigma models and tools in the deployment of continuous improvement in quality systems to help ensure compliance, efficiency, and effectiveness of the processes. Bautista Smith has a B.S. in chemical engineering from the University of Santo Tomas, a U.S. accredited university in the Philippines. Her ASQ certifications are: LSSBB (Black Belt), CQA, CQE, and CQM. Bautista Smith is also an ASQ instructor for CQA courses.

Bautista Smith's quality philosophy is embodied in her ASQ published books, *Auditing Beyond Compliance* and *The Art of Integrating Strategic Planning, Process Metrics, Risk Mitigation, and Auditing*. She is also very involved in the support of autism programs, depicted in her self-published book, *Nielda Is Different*.

In addition to Bautista Smith's hands-on manufacturing experience, she has provided tutorial classes in Auditing Beyond Compliance at several ASQ Audit Conferences and Purdue University in West Lafayette, Indiana. Bautista Smith performed supplier audits and supplier development activities, Green Belt courses, and international audits of manufacturing companies in Sweden, Japan, and Holland.

Bautista Smith's hobbies include painting using watercolor and alcohol ink. One of her art achievements is being "Artist of the Month" (March 2020) and exhibiting at the Earth Discovery Center, Eagle Creek Park, Indiana.

Robert Alvarez

Contributions on the auditor's perspective

Bringing more than 40 years' experience, Robert Alvarez focuses on the maintenance and implementation of management systems. His experience comprises technical writing, including EASA and FAR part 145 repair station applications. As a senior consultant, Alvarez has implemented several successful projects for the U. S. Department of Justice/Bureau of Prisons, the Federal Penitentiary System, and Naval Surface Warfare Centers. His specialized experience includes aircraft, motor vehicles, metal fabrication, and knowledge of special processes. Other qualifications include administration of training and proctoring examinations for Probitas/Exemplar Global Auditor programs. Alvarez also holds the following certifications: Certified auditor for ISO 9001, AS9100, ISO 14001, and ISO 45001; FAA—Designated Manufacturing Inspection Representative; ASNT Level 1 Certificate in Radiography; and Certified Automotive Technician—California Apprenticeship Council. Alvarez is an active member of ASQ and has held several managerial positions for major corporations, such as McDonnell Douglas Aircraft, Airbus, and Teledyne Aircraft products.